Learn Python:

A Crash Course On Python Programming And How To Start Coding With It.
Learn The Basics Of Machine Learning And Data Analysis

by Damon Parker

Table of Contents

Introduction

Congratulations on purchasing *Learn Python: A Crash Course On Python Programming And How To Start Coding With It. Learn The Basics Of Machine Learning And Data Analysis,* and thank you for doing so.

The following chapters will discuss the core concepts of Python coding to help you kick start your coding journey. You will also learn the fundamentals of data analysis and machine learning technology. You will start this book with the key features and advantages of learning to code Python as well as the history of how Python programming was created. In the first chapter of this book, you will find instructions on how to install Python on your operating systems (Windows, Mac, and Linux). The concept of Python data types is presented in exquisite detail with various examples of each data type. In Python, variables are at the heart of every syntax. You will learn how to create these variables and assign desired data type to them. This chapter also includes comprehensive lists of a variety of built-in functions and methods supported by Python.

The chapter 2 of this book titled "Python Coding" will introduce you to the basic concepts of writing efficient and effective Python codes, focusing on various programming elements such as Booleans, Tuples, Sets, Dictionaries and much more. Each concept is explained with standard syntax, relevant examples, and followed by exercises to help you test and verify your understanding of all the concepts. You will also learn how to write "if" and "else" statements to retrieve desired information from your data. The concept of "for" and "while" loops are explained with explicit details in an easy to understand language.

In chapter 3 titled Data Analysis and Machine Learning with Python, you will learn the basics of big data analysis and the fundamental machine learning algorithms. This chapter also includes brief overview of various renowned machine learning libraries such as Scikit-Learn, NumPy, Matplotlib, SymPy and Pandas among others. A detailed walkthrough with an open-source database using illustrations and actual Python code that you can try hands-on by following the instructions in this book. A number of Python coding tips and tricks have also been provided that will help you sharpen up your Python programming skillset or get familiar with the coding if you are new to Python coding.

There are plenty of books on this subject on the market, thanks again for choosing this one! Every effort was made to ensure it is full of as much useful information as possible; please enjoy!

Chapter 1: Introduction to Python

Python is a high-level programming language, commonly used for general purposes. It was originally developed by Guido van Rossum at the "Center Wiskunde & Informatica (CWI), Netherlands," in the 1980s and introduced by the "Python Software Foundation" in 1991. It was designed primarily to emphasize readability of programming code, and its syntax enables programmers to convey ideas using fewer lines of code. Python programming language increases the speed of operation while allowing for higher efficiency in creating system integrations. Developers are using Python for "web development (server-side), software development, mathematics, system scripting."

With the introduction of various enhancements such as "list comprehension" and a "garbage collection system," which can collect reference cycles, the Python 2.0 was launched in the last quarter of 2000. Subsequently, in 2008, Python 3.0 was released as a major version upgrade with backward compatibility allowing for the Python 2.0 code to be executed on Python 3.0 without requiring any modifications. Python is supported by a community of programmers that continually develop and maintain the "CPython", which is an open-source reference implementation. The "Python Software Foundation" is a not for profit organization that is responsible for managing and directing resources for developing Python programming as well as "CPython."

Here are some of the key features of Python that render it as the language of choice for coding beginners as well as advanced software programmers alike:

1. **Readability**: Python reads a lot like the English language, which contributes to its ease of readability.
2. **Learnability**: Python is a high level programming language and considered easy to learn due to the ability to code using English language like expressions, which implies it is simple to comprehend and thereby learn the language.
3. **Operating Systems**: Python is easily accessible and can be operated across different Operating systems including Linux, Unix, Mac, Windows among others. This renders Python as a versatile and cross-platform language.
4. **Open Source**: Python is "open source", which means that the developer community can seamlessly make updates to the code, which are always available to anyone using Python for their software programming needs.
5. **Standardized Data Libraries**: Python features a big standard data library with a variety of useful codes and

functionalities that can be used when writing Python code for data analysis and development of machine learning models. (Details on machine learning libraries will be provided later in this chapter)

6. **Free**: Considering the wide applicability and usage of Python, it is hard to believe that it continues to be freely available for easy download and use. This implies that anyone looking to learn or use Python can simply download and use it for their applications completely free of charge. Python is indeed a perfect example of a "FLOSS (Free/Libre Open Source Software)", which means one could "freely distribute copies of this software, read its source code and modify it."

7. **Supports managing of exceptions**: An "exception" can be defined as "an event that can occur during program exception and can disrupt the normal flow of program." Python is capable of supporting handling of these "exceptions," implying that you could write fewer error-prone codes and test your code with a variety of cases, which could potentially lead to an "exception" in the future.

8. **Advanced Features**: Python can also support "generators and list comprehensions."

9. **Storage governance**: Python is also able to support "automatic memory management," which implies that the

storage memory will be cleared and made available automatically. You are not required to clear and free up the system memory.

Applications:

1. Web designing – Some of the widely used web frameworks such as "Django" and "Flask" have been developed using Python. These frameworks assist the developer in writing server-side codes that enable management of database, generation of backend programming logic, mapping of URL, among others. Machine learning –A variety of machine learning models have been written exclusively in Python. Machine learning is a way for machines to write logic in order to learn and fix a specific issue on its own. For instance, Python-based machine learning algorithms used in development of "product recommendation systems" for eCommerce businesses such as Amazon, Netflix, YouTube and many more. Other instances of Python-based machine learning models are the facial recognition and the voice recognition technologies available on our mobile devices.

2. Data Analysis–Python can also be used in the development of data visualization and data analysis tools and techniques such as scatter plots and other graphical representations of data.

3. "Scripting" –It can be defined as the process of generating simple programs for automation of straightforward tasks like those required to send automated email responses and text messages. You could develop these types of software using the Python programming language.

4. Gaming Industry –A wide variety of gaming programs have been developed with the use of Python.

5. Python also supports the development of "embedded applications."

6. Desktop apps–You could use data libraries such as "TKinter" or "QT" to create desktop apps based on Python.

Installation Instructions for Python

You can follow the step by step instructions to download and install Python on a variety of operating systems. Simply jump to the section for the operating system you are working on. The latest version of Python released in the middle of the 2019 is Python 3.8.0. Make sure you are downloading and installing the most recent and stable version of Python and following the instructions in the following pages.

WINDOWS

1. From the official Python website, click on the "Downloads" icon and select Windows.
2. Click on the "Download Python 3.8.0" button to view all the downloadable files.
3. You will be taken to a different screen where you can select the Python version you would like to download. In this book, we will be using the Python 3 version under "Stable Releases." So scroll down the page and click on the "Download Windows x86-64 executable installer" link as shown in the picture below.

- Python 3.8.0 - Oct. 14, 2019
  Note that Python 3.8.0 *cannot* be used on Windows XP or earlier.

  - Download Windows help file
  - Download Windows x86-64 embeddable zip file
  - Download Windows x86-64 executable installer
  - Download Windows x86-64 web-based installer
  - Download Windows x86 embeddable zip file
  - Download Windows x86 executable installer
  - Download Windows x86 web-based installer

4. A pop-up window titled "python-3.8.0-amd64.exe" will be displayed.
5. Click on the "Save File" button to start downloading the file.
6. Once the download has completed, double click the saved file icon, and a "Python 3.8.0 (64-bit) Setup" pop window will be displayed.

7. Make sure that you select the "Install Launcher for all users (recommended)" and the "Add Python 3.8 to PATH" checkboxes. Note – If you already have an older version of Python installed on your system, the "Upgrade Now" button will appear instead of the "Install Now" button, and neither of the checkboxes will be displayed.

8. Click on the "Install Now" button and a "User Account Control" pop up window will be displayed.

9. A notification stating, "Do you want to allow this app to make changed to your device" will be displayed, click on Yes.

10. A new pop up window titled "Python 3.8.0 (64-bit) Setup" will be displayed containing a setup progress bar.

11. Once the installation has been completed, a "Set was successful" message will be displayed. Click on the Close button, and you are all set.

12. To verify the installation, navigate to the directory where you installed Python and double click on the python.exe file.

MACINTOSH

1. From the official Python website, click on the "Downloads" icon and select Mac.

2. Click on the "Download Python 3.8.0" button to view all the downloadable files.

3. You will be taken to a different screen where you can select the Python version you would like to download. In this book, we will be using the Python 3 version under "Stable Releases." So scroll down the page and click on the "Download macOS 64-bit installer" link under Python 3.8.0, as shown in the picture below.

- Python 3.7.5 - Oct. 15, 2019
  - Download macOS 64-bit/32-bit installer
  - Download macOS 64-bit installer
- Python 3.8.0 - Oct. 14, 2019
  - Download macOS 64-bit installer
- Python 3.7.4 - July 8, 2019
  - Download macOS 64-bit/32-bit installer
  - Download macOS 64-bit installer
- Python 3.6.9 - July 2, 2019

4. A pop-up window titled "python-3.8.0-macosx10.9.pkg" will be displayed.

5. Click on the "Save File" button to start downloading the file.

6. Once the download has completed, double click the saved file icon, and an "Install Python" pop window will be displayed.

7. Click on the "Continue" button to proceed, and a terms and conditions pop up window will be displayed.

8. Click Agree and then click on the "Install" button.

9. A notification requesting administrator permission and password will be displayed. Simply enter your system password to begin installation.

10. Once the installation has been completed, an "Installation was successful" message will be displayed. Click on the Close button, and you are all set.

11. To verify the installation, navigate to the directory where you installed Python and double click on the python launcher icon that will take you to the Python Terminal.

LINUX

- **For Red Hat, CentOS, or Fedora**, install the python3 and python3-devel packages.
- **For Debian or Ubuntu**, install the python3.x and python3.x-dev packages.
- **For Gentoo**, install the '=python-3.x*' ebuild (you may have to unmask it first).

1. From the official Python website, click on the "Downloads" icon and select Linux/UNIX.

2. Click on the "Download Python 3.8.0" button to view all the downloadable files.

3. You will be taken to a different screen where you can select the Python version you would like to download. In this book, we will be using the Python 3 version under "Stable Releases." So scroll down the page and click on the "Download Gzipped source tarball" link under Python 3.8.0, as shown in the picture below.

4. A pop-up window titled "python-3.7.5.tgz" will be displayed.

5. Click on the "Save File" button to start downloading the file.

6. Once the download has completed, double click the saved file icon, and an "Install Python" pop window will be displayed.

7. Follow the prompts on the screen to complete the installation process.

Getting Started

Now that you have the Python terminal installed on your computer, we will now see how you can start writing and executing the Python code. All Python codes are written in a text editor as (.py) files, which are then executed on the Python interpreter on the command line as shown in the code below, where "smallworld.py" is the name of the Python file:

"C: \Users\Your Name\python smallworld.py"

You can test a small code without writing the code in a file and simply executing it as a command-line itself by typing the code below on the Mac, Windows or Linux command line, as shown below:

"C: \Users\Your Name\python"

In case the above command doesn't work, you can use the code below instead

"C: \Users\Your Name\py"

Indentation – To understand the Python coding structure, you must first understand the significance of indentation or the number of spaces before you start typing the code. Unlike other coding languages where "indentation" is added to enhance the readability of the code, in Python, it is used to indicate a set of code. For example, look at the code below

If 6 > 3:
        print ('Six is greater than 3')
There is indentation prior to the second line of code with the print command. If you skip the indentation and write the code as below, you will receive an error:

If 6 > 3:

19

print ('Six is greater than 3')

The number of spaces can be adjusted but must be at least single-spaced. For example, you can execute the code below with higher indentation, but for a specific set of code same number of spaces must be used, or you will receive an error.

If 6 > 3:

        print ('Six is greater than 3')

Adding Comments – In Python, you can add comments to the code by starting the code comment lines with a "#", as shown in the example below:

#Add any relevant comment here
print ('Small World)

Comments are also used as a description of the code and not executed by the Python terminal. It is important to remember that if you put a comment at the end of code like the entire code line will be skipped by the Python terminal as shown in the code below. Comments are extremely useful in case you need to stop the execution when you are testing the code.

print ('Small World')   *#Add comments here*

You can also add multiple lines of comments by starting each code line with "#," as shown below:

#Add comment here
#Supplement the comment here
#Further add the comment here
print ('Small World')

Python Variables

In Python, variables are used to store data values without executing a command for it. You can create a variable by simply assigning desired value to it, as shown in the example below:

A = 100
B = 'Patrick'
print (A)
print (B)

A variable may be declared without a specific data type. The data type of a variable can also be modified after it's initial declaration, as shown in the example below:

A = 100 # A has data type set as int
A = 'Nick' # A now has data type str
print (A)

There are certain rules applied to the Python variable names as follows:

1. Variable names can be short as single alphabets or more descriptive words like height, weight, etc
2. Variable names can only be started with an underscore character or a letter.
3. Variable names must not start with numbers.
4. Variable names may contain underscores or alphanumeric characters. No other special characters are allowed.
5. Variable names are case sensitive. For example, 'height,' 'Height' and 'HEIGHT' will be accounted as 3 separate variables.

Assigning Value to Variables

In Python, multiple variables can be assigned DISTINCT values in a single code line, as shown in the example below:

A, B, C = 'purple,' 'red,' 'blue'
print (A)
print (B)
print (C)

OR multiple variables can be assigned SAME value in a single code line, as shown in the example below:

A, B, C = '*purple*'
print (A)
print (B)
print (C)

Python Data Types

To further understand the concept of variables, let's first look at the Python data types. Python supports a variety of data types as listed below:

Category	Data Type	Example Syntax
Text	*"str"*	'Small World' "Small World" """Small World"""
Boolean	*"bool"*	'True' 'False'
Mapping (mixed data types, associative array of key and value pairs)	*"dict"*	'{'key9' : 9.0, 6 : True}'

Sequence (may contain mixed data types)	*"list"*	'[9.0, 'character', True]'
	"tuple"	'[9.0, 'character', True]'
	"range"	'range (10, 50)' 'range (100, 50, 10, -10, -50, -100)'
Binary	*"bytes"*	b 'byte sequence' b 'byte sequence' bytes ([120, 90, 75, 100])
	"bytearray"	bytearray (b 'byte sequence') bytearray (b 'byte sequence') bytearray ([120, 90, 75, 100])
	"memoryview"	
Set (unordered, no duplicates, mixed data types)	*"set"*	'[9.0, 'character', True]'
	"frozenset"	'frozenset ([9.0, 'character', True])'
Numeric	*"int"*	'54'

Numeric	*"float"*	'18e9'
	"complex"	'18 + 3.1j'
Ellipsis (index in NumPy arrays)	*"ellipsis"*	'...' 'Ellipsis'

To view the data type of any object, you can use the *"type ()"* function as shown in the example below:

A = 'Purple'
print (type (A))

Assigning the Data Type to Variables

As mentioned earlier, you can create a new variable by simply declaring a value for it. This set data value, in turn, assigns the data type to the variable.

To assign a specific data type to a variable, the constructor functions listed below can be used:

Constructor Functions	**Data Type**
A = str ('Small World)'	str

A = int (99)	Int (Must be a whole number, positive or negative with no decimals, no length restrictions)
A = float (15e6)	Float (Floating point number must be a positive or negative number with one or more decimals; maybe scientific number an 'e' to specify an exponential power of 10)
A = complex (99j)	Complex (Must be written with a 'j' as an imaginary character)
A = list (('blue', 'red', 'green'))	list
A = range (1, 100)	range
A = tuple (('blue', 'red', 'green'))	tuple
A = set (('blue', 'red', 'green'))	set
A = frozenset (('blue', 'green', 'red'))	frozenset
A = dict ('color' : 'red', 'year' : 1999)	dict

A = bool (False)	bool
A = bytes (54)	bytes
A = bytearray (8)	bytearray
A = memoryview (bytes (55))	memoryview

EXERCISE – To solidify your understanding of data types. Look at the first column of the table below and write the data type for that variable. Once you have all your answers, look at the second column, and verify your answers.

Variable	Data Type
A = 'Small World'	str
A = 99	int
A = 29e2	float
A = 99j	complex
A = ['blue', 'red', 'green']	list
A = range (1, 100)	range
A = ('blue', 'red', 'green')	tuple
A = {'blue', 'red', 'green'}	set
A = frozenset ({ 'blue', 'green', 'red'})	frozenset
A = ['color' : 'red', 'year' : 1999}	dict
A = False	bool
A = b 'Welcome'	bytes
A = bytearray (8)	bytearray

A = *memoryview (bytes (55))*	memoryview

Output Variables

In order to retrieve variables as output, the "print" statements are used in Python. You can use the "+" character to combine text with a variable for final output, as shown in the example below:

'A = 'red'
print ('Apples are' + A)'

OUTPUT – 'Apples are red'

A variable can also be combined with another variable using the "+" character as shown in the example below:

'A = 'Apples are'
B = 'red'
AB = A + B
print (AB)'

OUTPUT – 'Apples are red'

However, when the "+" character is used with numeric values, it retains it's function as a mathematical operator, as shown in the example below:

'A = 20
B = 30
print (A + B)'

OUTPUT = 50

You will not be able to combine a string of characters with numbers and will trigger an error instead, as shown in the example below:

A = 'red'
B = 30
print (A + B)

OUTPUT – N/A – ERROR

Python Built-in Functions

Like most programming languages, Python boasts a number of built-in functions to make your life easier while coding a software program. Here is a list of all such built-in functions:

Function	Description
abs ()	Will result in the absolute values of the numbers.
all ()	Will result in True if all items within an iterative object are true.
any ()	Will result in True if any item of the iterative object holds true.
ascii ()	Will result in a readable version of an object and replace non-ascii characters with escape characters.
bin ()	Will result in the binary version of the numbers.
bool ()	Will result in the boolean values of indicated objects.
bytearray ()	Will result in an array of bytes.
bytes ()	Will result in bytes objects.
callable ()	Will result in True if a specific object is callable or else results in False.
chr ()	Will result in a character from the indicated Unicode code.
classmethod ()	Will convert any method into class method.
compile ()	Will result in the indicated source as an object, ready for execution.
complex ()	Will result in a complex number.

delattr ()	Will delete specific attributes (property or method) from the indicated object.
dict ()	Will result in a dictionary.
dir ()	Will result in a list of properties and methods of the specific object.
divmod ()	Will result in the quotient and the remainder when one argument is divided by another.
enumerate ()	Will take a collection and result in enumerate objects.
eval ()	Will evaluate and execute an expression.
exec ()	Will execute the indicated code (or object)
filter ()	Uses a filter function to exclude items in an iterative object.
float ()	Will result in floating point numbers.
format ()	Will format the indicated value.
frozenset ()	Will result in a frozen set object.
getattr ()	Will result in the value of the indicated attribute (property or method).
globals ()	Will result in the most recent global symbol table as a dictionary.
hasattr ()	Will result in True if the indicated

	object has the indicated attribute.
hash ()	Will result in the hash value of the indicated object.
help ()	Will execute the built-in help system.
hex ()	Conversion of numbers into hexadecimal values.
id ()	Will result in the identity of an object.
input ()	Will allow user input.
int ()	Will result in an integer number.
isinstance ()	Will result in True if the indicated object is an instance of the indicated object.
issubclass ()	Will result in True if the indicated class is a subclass of the indicated object.
iter ()	Will result in an iterative object.
len ()	Will result in the length of an object.
list ()	Will result in a list.
locals ()	Will result in an updated dictionary of the current local symbol table.
map ()	Will result in the indicated iterator with the indicated function applied to each item.
max ()	Will result in the largest item of an iteration.
memoryview ()	Will result in memory view objects.

min ()	Will result in the smallest item of an iteration.
next ()	Will result in the next item in an iteration.
object ()	Will result in a new object.
oct ()	Converts a number into an octet.
open ()	Will open files and result in file objects.
ord ()	Conversion of an integer representing the Unicode of the indicated character.
pow ()	Will result in the value of a to the power of b.
print ()	Will print to the standard output device.
property ()	Will retrieve, set, and delete a property.
range ()	Will result in a sequence of numbers, beginning from 0 and default increments of 1.
repr ()	Will result in a readable version of objects.
reversed ()	Will result in a reversed iteration.
round ()	Rounding of a number.
set ()	Will result in new set objects.

setattr ()	Will set attributes of the objects.
slice ()	Will result in a sliced objects.
sorted ()	Will result in sorted lists.
staticmethod ()	Will convert methods into a static method.
str ()	Will result in string objects.
sum ()	Will sum the items of iterations.
super ()	Will result in an object representing the parent class.
tuple ()	Will result in tuples.
type ()	Will result in the type of objects.
vars ()	Will result in the _dict_ property of objects.
zip ()	Will result in a single iteration from multiple iterations.

Python Built-in String methods

There are a number of built-in Python methods specifically for strings of data, which will result in new values for the string without making any changes to the original string. Here is a list of all such methods.

Method	Description
capitalize ()	Will convert the initial character to upper case.
casefold ()	Will convert strings into lower case.
center ()	Will result in centered strings.
count ()	Will result in the number of times an indicated value appears in a string.
encode ()	Will result in an encoded version of the strings.
endswith ()	Will result in true if the string ends with the indicated value.
expandtabs ()	Will set the tab size of the string.
find ()	Will search the string for indicated value and result in its position.
format ()	Will format indicated values of strings.
format_map ()	Will format indicated values of strings.
index ()	Will search the string for indicated value and result in its position.
isalnum ()	Will result in True if all string characters are alphanumeric.
isalpha ()	Will result in True if all string characters are alphabets.

isdecimal ()	Will result in True if all string characters are decimals.
isdigit ()	Will result in True if all string characters are digits.
isidentifier ()	Will result in True if the strings is an identifier.
islower ()	Will result in True if all string characters are lower case.
isnumeric ()	Will result in True if all string characters are numeric.
isprintable ()	Will result in True if all string characters are printable.
isspace ()	Will result in True if all string characters are whitespaces.
istitle ()	Will result in True if the string follows the rules of a title.
isupper ()	Will result in True if all string characters are upper case.
join ()	Will join the elements of an iteration to the end of the string.
ljust ()	Will result in a left-justified version of the string.
lower ()	Will convert a string into lower case.
lstrip ()	Will result in a left trim version of the string.

maketrans ()	Will result in a translation table to be used in translations.
partition ()	Will result in a tuple where the string is separated into 3 sections.
replace ()	Will result in a string where an indicated value is replaced with another indicated value.
rfind ()	Will search the string for an indicated value and result in its last position.
rindex ()	Will search the string for an indicated value and result in its last position.
rjust ()	Will result in the right justified version of the string.
rpartition ()	Will result in a tuple where the string is separated into 3 sections.
rsplit ()	Will split the string at the indicated separator and result in a list.
rstrip ()	Will result in a new string version that has been trimmed at its right.
split ()	Will split the string at the indicated separator and result in a list.
splitlines ()	Will split the string at line breaks and result in a list.

startswith ()	Will result in true if the string starts with the indicated value.
strip ()	Will result in a trimmed version of the string.
swapcase ()	Will swap the alphabet cases.
title ()	Will convert the first character of each word to upper case.
translate ()	Will result in a translated string.
upper ()	Will convert a string into upper case.
zfill ()	Will fill the string with the indicated number of 0 values at the beginning.

Python Random Numbers

A "random ()" function does not exist in Python, but it has an embedded module called "random" that may be utilized to create numbers randomly when needed. For instance, if you wanted to call the "random" module and display a number randomly between 100 and 500, you can accomplish this by executing the code below:

import random
print (random.randrange (100, 500))

OUTPUT – Any number between 100 and 500 will be randomly displayed.

There are a number of defined methods in the random module as listed below:

Method	Description
betavariate ()	Will result in random float numbers between 0 and 1 based on the Beta distribution.
choice ()	Will result in random elements on the basis of the provided sequence.
choices ()	Will result in a list consisting of a random selection from the provided sequence.
expovariate ()	Will result in a float number randomly displayed between 0 and -1, or between 0 and 1 for negative parameters on the basis of the statistical exponential distributions.
gammavariate ()	Will result in a float number displayed between 0 and 1 on the basis of the statistical Gamma distribution.
gauss ()	Will result in a float number displayed between 0 and 1 on the

	basis of the Gaussian distribution, which is widely utilized in probability theory.
getrandbits ()	Will result in a number that represents the random bits.
getstate ()	Will result in the current internal state of the random number generator.
lognormvariate ()	Will result in a float number randomly displayed between 0 and 1 on the basis of a log-normal distribution, which is widely utilized in probability theory.
normalvariate()	Will result in a float number randomly displayed between 0 and 1 on the basis of the normal distribution, which is widely utilized in probability theory.
paretovariate()	Will result in a float number randomly displayed between 0 and 1 on the basis of the Pareto distribution, which is widely utilized in probability theory.
randint ()	Will result in a random number between the provided range.

random ()	Will result in a float number randomly displayed between 0 and 1.
randrange ()	Will result in a random number between the provided range.
sample ()	Will result in a sample of the sequences.
seed ()	Will trigger the random number generator.
setstate ()	Will restore the internal state of the random number generator.
shuffle ()	Will take a sequence and result in a sequence but in some random order.
triangular ()	Will result in a random float number between two provided parameters. You could also set a mode parameter for specification of the midpoint between the two other parameters.
uniform ()	Will result in a random float number between two provided parameters.
vonmisesvariate()	Will result in a float number randomly displayed between 0 and 1 on the basis of the von "Mises distribution", which is utilized in directional statistics.
weibullvariate()	Will result in a float number randomly displayed between 0 and 1

	on the basis of the Weibull distribution, which is utilized in statistics.

Python Built-in List methods

Python supports a number of built-in methods that can be used on lists or arrays, as listed in the table below:

Method	Description
append ()	Will insert an element at the end of the list.
clear ()	Will remove all the list elements.
copy ()	Will result in a replica of the list.
count ()	Will result in the number of elements with the indicated value.
extend ()	Will add the elements of a list (or any iterator), to the end of the current list.
index ()	Will result in the index of the first element with the indicated value.
insert ()	Will add an element at the indicated position.
pop ()	Will remove the element at the indicated position.
remove ()	Will remove the first item with the indicated value.

reverse ()	Will reverse the order of the list.
sort ()	Will sort the list.

Python Built-in Tuple methods

Python supports a couple of built-in methods that can be used on tuples, as listed in the table below:

Method	Description
count ()	Will result in the number of times an indicated value appears in the tuple.
index ()	Will search a tuple for the indicated value and result in the position of where the value is found.

Python Built-in Set methods

Python also supports a variety of embedded methods that can be used on sets that are listed in the table below:

Method	Description
"add ()"	Will add an element to the set.
"clear ()"	Will remove all the elements from the set.
"copy ()"	Will result in a replica of the set.
"difference ()"	Will result in a set that contains the difference between 2 or more sets.

"difference_update ()"	Will remove the items from a set that can be found in another, indicated set.
"discard ()"	Will remove the indicated item.
"intersection ()"	Will result in a set that is the intersection of couple other sets.
"intersection_update ()"	Will remove the items from a set that are not present in another indicated set.
"isdisjoint ()"	Will determine if intersection exists between two sets.
"issubset ()"	Will determine if the identified set contains another set.
"issuperset ()"	Will determine if a different set contain the identified set or not.
"pop ()"	Will remove an element from the set.
"remove ()"	Will remove the indicated element.
"symmetric_difference ()"	Will result in a set with the symmetric differences of the two indicated sets.
"symmetric_difference _update ()"	Will insert the symmetric differences from the indicated set and other sets.

"union ()"	Will result in a set containing the union of sets.
"update ()"	Will update the set with the union of the indicated set and other sets.

Python Built-in Dictionary methods

Python also supports a large number of built-in methods that can be used on dictionaries that are listed in the table below:

Method	Description
clear ()	Will remove all the elements from the dictionary.
copy ()	Will result in a copy of the dictionary.
fromkeys ()	Will result in a dictionary with the indicated keys and values.
get ()	Will result in the values of the indicated key.
items ()	Will result in a list containing a tuple for every key-value pair.
keys ()	Will result in a list containing the keys of the dictionary.
pop ()	Will remove the elements with the indicated key.
popitem ()	Will remove the key value pair that was most recently added.

setdefault ()	Will result in the values of the indicated key. In case the key is not found, a new key will be added with the indicated values.
update ()	Will update the dictionary with the indicated key value pairs.
values ()	Will result in a list of all the values in the dictionary.

Python Built-in File methods

Python also supports a large number of built-in methods that can be used on file objects that are listed in the table below:

Method	Description
close ()	Will close the file
detach ()	Will result in a separate raw stream.
fileno ()	Will result in a number representing the stream, per the operating system processing.
flush ()	Will flush the internal buffer.
isatty ()	Will result in determination if the file stream is interactive.
read ()	Will result in the content of the file.
readable ()	Will result in determination if the file stream is readable or not.

readline ()	Will result in one line from the file.
readlines ()	Will result in a list of lines from the file.
seek ()	Will modify the position of the file.
seekable ()	Will result in determination if the file permits modification of its position.
tell ()	Will result in the current position of the file.
truncate ()	Will change the size of the file to the indicated value.
writeable ()	Will result in determination if the file permits writing over.
write ()	Will write the indicated string to the file.
writelines ()	Will writes a list of strings to the file.

Python Keywords

Python contains some keywords that cannot be used to define a variable or used as a function name or any other unique identifier. These select Python keywords are listed in the table below:

Method	Description
"and"	Logical operator.
"as"	For creating an alias.
"assert"	To debug.
"break"	For breaking out of a loop.

"class"	For defining a class.
"continue"	For continuing to the next iteration of a loop.
"def"	For defining a function.
"del"	For deleting an object.
"elif"	For use in conditional statements, similar to "else if".
"else"	For use in conditional statements.
"except"	For use with exceptions, so the program knows the steps to follow in case of an exception.
"FALSE"	One of the data values assigned only to Boolean data type.
"finally"	For use with exceptions, this set of code would be executed regardless of any occurrences of an exception.
"for"	Used in creation of a "for loop".
"from"	For importing particular part of a module.
"global"	For declaring a global variable.
"if"	For making conditional statements.
"import"	For importing desired module.
"in"	For checking a specific data value within a tuple or a list.
"is"	For testing two variables that may be equal.
"lambda"	For creating an anonymous function.

"None"	For representation of null data value.
"nonlocal"	For declaration of a non-local variable.
"not"	Logical operator.
"or"	Logical operator.
"pass"	Will result in a null statement that would not be executed.
"raise"	Used to raise an exception to the statement.
"result in"	Used for exiting a function and resulting in a data value.
"TRUE"	One of the data values assigned only to Boolean data type.
"try"	Used for making "try except" statements.
"while"	For creating a "while loop".
"with"	Used for simplification of the handling procedure for exceptions.
"yield"	For terminating a function and resulting in a generator.

Chapter 2: Python Coding

In the previous chapter, you learned the basics of Python syntax, the concept of Python Variables and Comments, as well as details of various built-in Python methods and keywords that serve as a prerequisite to the learning of Python programming. In this chapter, we will be looking at the nuances of how to write efficient and effective Python codes, focusing on various programming elements such as Booleans, Tuples, Sets, Dictionaries and much more. So let's get started.

Python Numbers

In Python programming, you will be working with 3 different numeric data types, namely, "int," "float" and "complex." In the previous chapter, you learned the details of what these data types entail, but below are some examples to refresh your memory.

Data Type	Example
Int (Must be a whole number, positive or negative with no decimals, no length restrictions)	*36 or 3.14*

Float (Floating point number must be a positive or negative number with one or more decimals; maybe scientific number an "e" to specify an exponential power of 10)	29e5
Complex (Must be written with a "j" as an imaginary character)	99j

EXERCISE – Create variable "a" with data value as "3.14", variable "b" with data value as "9e2" and variable "c" with data value as "-29j".

USE YOUR DISCRETION HERE AND WRITE YOUR CODE FIRST

Now, check your code against the correct code below:

```
a = 3.14        # int
b = 9e2         # float
c = -29j        # complex
```

```
print (type (a))
print (type (b))
print (type (c))
```

Note – The # comments are not required for the correct code and are only mentioned to bolster your understanding of the concept.

Converting one numeric data type to another

As all Python variables are dynamic in nature, you will be able to convert the data type of these variables if needed by deriving a new variable from the variable that you would like to assign a new data type.

Let's continue building on the exercise discussed above.

```
a = 3.14      # int
b = 9e2       # float
c = -29j      # complex

#conversion from int to float
x = float (a)

#conversion from float to complex
y = complex (b)
```

```
#conversion from complex to int
z = float (c)


#conversion from int to complex
x1 = int (a)


print (x)
print (y)
print (z)
print (x1)


print (type (x))
print (type (y))
print (type (z))
print (type (x1))
```

EXERCISE – View a random number between 10 and 20 by importing the random module.

USE YOUR DISCRETION HERE AND WRITE YOUR CODE FIRST

Now, check your code against the correct code below:

```
import random
print (random.randrange (10, 20))
```

Variable Casting with Constructor Functions

In the discussion and exercise above, you learned that variables could be declared by simply assigning desired data value to them and thereby the variables will assume the pertinent data type based on the data value. However, Python allows you to specify the data types for variables by using classes or "constructor functions" to define the data type for variables. This process is called "Casting."

Here are the 3 constructor functions used for "casting" numeric data type to a variable.

Constructor Functions	Data Type
int ()	Will construct an integer number from an integer literal, a string literal (provided the string is representing a whole number) or a float literal (by rounding down to the preceding whole number)
float ()	Will construct a float number from a string literal (provided the string is representing a float or an integer), a float literal or an integer literal

complex ()	Will construct a string from a large number of data types, such as integer literals, float literals, and strings

Here are some examples:

Integer:

a = int (5)   # a takes the value 5
b = int (3.6)   # b takes the value 3
c = int ('4')   # c takes the value 4

Float:

a = float (5)   # a takes the value 5.0
b = float (3.6)   # b takes the value 3.6
c = float ('4')   # c takes the value 4.0

String:

a = str ('serial')   # a takes the value 'serial'
b = str (3.6)   # b takes the value '3.6'
c = str ('4')   # c takes the value '4.0'

Python Strings

In Python, string data type for a variable is denoted by using single, double, or triple quotation marks. This implies that you can assign string data value to variable by quoting the string of characters. For example, "welcome" is the same as 'welcome' and "'welcome'".

EXERCISE – Create a variable "v" with a string data value as "sky is blue" and display it.

USE YOUR DISCRETION HERE AND WRITE YOUR CODE FIRST

Now, check your code against the correct code below:

v = 'sky is blue'
print (v)

OUTPUT – sky is blue

EXERCISE – Create a variable "A" with a multiple-line string data value as "Looking at the sky tonight, thinking of you by my side! Let the world go on and on, it will be alright if I stay strong!" and display it.

USE YOUR DISCRETION HERE AND WRITE YOUR CODE FIRST

Now, check your code against the correct code below:

```
a = """Looking at the sky tonight,
thinking of you by my side!
Let the world go on and on,
it will be alright if I stay strong!"""
print (a)
```

OUTPUT – Looking at the sky tonight,
thinking of you by my side!
Let the world go on and on,
it will be alright if I stay strong!

Note – You must use triple quote to create multiline string data values.

String Arrays

In Python, string data values are arrays of bytes that represent Unicode characters as true for most programming languages. But unlike other programming languages, Python lacks data type for individual characters, which are denoted as string data type with length of 1.

The first character of every string is given the position of 'o', and subsequently the subsequent characters will have the position as

1, 2, 3, and so on. In order to display desired characters from a string data value, you can use the position of the character enclosed in square brackets. For example, if you wanted to display the fifth character of the string data value "apple" of variable "x." You will use the command "print (x [4])"

EXERCISE – Create a variable "P" with a string data value as "awesome" and display the fourth character of this string.

USE YOUR DISCRETION HERE AND WRITE YOUR CODE FIRST

Now, check your code against the correct code below:

P = 'awesome'
print (P [3])

OUTPUT – s

Slicing

If you would like to view a range of characters, you can do so by specifying the start and the end index of the desired positions and separating the indexes by a colon. For example, to view characters of a string from position 1 to position 3, your code will be *"print (variable [1:3])"*.

You can even view the characters starting from the end of the string by using "negative indexes" and start slicing the string from the end of the string. For example, to view characters of a string from position 4 to position 1, your code will be *"print (variable [-4 : -2])"*.

In order to view the length of the string, you can use the "len ()" function. For example, to view the length of a string, your code will be *"print (len (variable))."*

EXERCISE – Create a variable "P" with a string data value as "roses are red!" and display characters from position 3 to 6 of this string.

USE YOUR DISCRETION HERE AND WRITE YOUR CODE FIRST

Now, check your code against the correct code below:

P = 'roses are red!'
print (P [3 : 6])

OUTPUT – esa

EXERCISE – Create a variable "x" with a string data value as "python is easy" and display characters from position 5 to 1, starting the count from the end of this string.

USE YOUR DISCRETION HERE AND WRITE YOUR CODE FIRST

Now, check your code against the correct code below:

x = 'python is easy'
print (x [-5 : -2])

OUTPUT - sea

EXERCISE – Create a variable "z" with a string data value as "coding beginner" and display the length of this string.

USE YOUR DISCRETION HERE AND WRITE YOUR CODE FIRST

Now, check your code against the correct code below:

z = 'coding beginner'
print (len (z))

OUTPUT - 14

String Methods

There are various built-in methods in Python that can be applied to string data values. Here are the Python codes for some of the most frequently used string methods, using variable *"P = 'roses are red!'"*.

"strip ()" method – To remove any blank spaces at the start and the end of the string.

P = "   roses are red!   "
print (P.strip ())

OUTPUT – roses are red!

"lower ()" method – To result in all the characters of a string in lower case.

P = "ROSES are RED!"
print (P.lower ())

OUTPUT – roses are red!

"upper ()" method – To result in all the characters of a string in upper case.

P = "Roses are Red!"

print (P.upper ())

OUTPUT – ROSES ARE RED!

"replace ()" method – To replace select characters of a string.

P = "roses are red!"

print (P.replace ("roses", "apples"))

OUTPUT – apples are red!

"split ()" method – To split a string into substrings using comma as the separator.

P = "Roses, Apples"

print (P.split (","))

OUTPUT – ['Roses', 'Apples']

String Concatenation

There might be instances when you need to collate different string variables. This can be accomplished with the use of the "+" logical operator. Here's the syntax for this Python code:

X = "string1"

Y = "string2"

$Z = X + Y$

print (Z)

Similarly, below is the syntax to insert a blank space between two different string variables.

$X = $ *"string1"*
$Y = $ *"string2"*
$Z = X + $ *" "* $ + Y$
print (Z)

However, Python does not permit the concatenation of string variables with numeric variables. But can be accomplished with the use of the *"format ()"* method, which will format the executed arguments and place them in the string where the placeholders "{ }" are used. Here's the syntax for this Python code:

$X = $ *numeric*
$Y = $ *"String"*
print (Y. format (X))

EXERCISE – Create two variables "A" and "B" with string data values as "I love" and "my country!" and display them as a concatenated string.

USE YOUR DISCRETION HERE AND WRITE YOUR CODE FIRST

Now, check your code against the correct code below:

```
A = "I love"
B = "my country!"
C = A + B
print (C)
```

OUTPUT – I love my country!

EXERCISE – Create two variables "A" with string data values as "my lucky number is" and "B" with numeric data value as "333" and display them as a concatenated string.

USE YOUR DISCRETION HERE AND WRITE YOUR CODE FIRST

Now, check your code against the correct code below:

```
A = "my lucky number is"
B = "333"
print (A. format (B))
```

OUTPUT – my lucky number is 333

Python Booleans

In the process of developing a software program, there is often a need to confirm and verify whether an expression is true or false. This is where Python Boolean data type and data values are used. In Python, comparison and evaluation of two data values will result in one of the two Boolean values: "True" or "False."

Here are some examples of comparison statement of numeric data leading to Boolean value:

print (100 > 90)

OUTPUT – True

print (100 == 90)

OUTPUT – False

print (100 < 90)

OUTPUT – False

66

Let's look at the *"bool ()"* function now, which allows for evaluation of numeric data as well as string data resulting in "True" or "False" Boolean values.

print (bool (99))

OUTPUT - True

print (bool ("Welcome"))

OUTPUT - True

Here are some key points to remember for Booleans:

1. If a statement has some kind of content, it would be evaluated as "True."
2. All string data values will be result ined as "True" unless the string is empty.
3. All numeric values will be result ined as "True" except "0"
4. Lists, Tuples, Set and Dictionaries will be result ined as "True", unless they are empty.
5. Mostly empty values like (), [], {}, "", False, None and 0 will be result ined as "False".
6. Any object created with the "_len_" function that result in the data value as "0" or "False" will be evaluated as "False".

In Python there are various built-in functions function that can be evaluated as Boolean, for example, the "isinstance()" function which allows you to determine the data type of an object. Therefore, in order to check if an object is integer, the code will be as below:

X = 10

print (isinstance (X, int))

EXERCISE – Create two variables "X" with string data values as "Yes I can!" and "Y" with numeric data value as "3.14" and evaluate them.

USE YOUR DISCRETION HERE AND WRITE YOUR CODE FIRST

Now, check your code against the correct code below:

X = "Yes I can!"
Y = 3.14
print (bool (X))
print (bool (Y)

OUTPUT –
True
True

Python Lists

In Python, lists are collections of data types that can be changed, organized and include duplicate values. Lists are written within square brackets, as shown in the syntax below.

X = ["string1", "string2", "string3"]
print (X)

The same concept of position applies to Lists as the string data type, which dictates that the first string is considered to be at position 0. Subsequently, the strings that will follow are given position 1, 2 and so on. You can selectively display desired string from a List by referencing the position of that string inside square bracket in the print command as shown below.

X = ["string1", "string2", "string3"]
print (X [2])

OUTPUT – [string3]

Similarly, the concept of **negative indexing** is also applied to Python List. Let's look at the example below:

X = ["string1", "string2", "string3"]
print (X [-2])

OUTPUT – [string2]

You will also be able to specify a **range of indexes** by indicating the start and end of a range. The result in values of such command on a Python List would be a new List containing only the indicated items. Here is an example for your reference.

X = ["string1", "string2", "string3", "string4", "string5", "string6"]
print (X [2 : 4])

OUTPUT – ["string3", "string4"]

* Remember the first item is at position 0, and the final position of the range (4) is not included.

Now, if you do not indicate the start of this range, it will default to the position 0 as shown in the example below:

X = ["string1", "string2", "string3", "string4", "string5", "string6"]
print (X [: 3])

OUTPUT – ["string1", "string2", "string3"]

Similarly, if you do not indicate the end of this range it will display all the items of the List from the indicated start range to the end of the List, as shown in the example below:

X = ["string1", "string2", "string3", "string4", "string5",
"string6"]
print (X [3 :])

OUTPUT – ["string4", "string5", "string6"]

You can also specify a **range of negative indexes** to Python Lists, as shown in the example below:

X = ["string1", "string2", "string3", "string4", "string5",
"string6"]
print (X [-3 : -1])

OUTPUT – ["string4", "string5"]

* Remember the last item is at position -1, and the final position of this range (-1) is not included in the Output.

There might be instances when you need to **change the data value** for a Python List. This can be accomplished by referring to the index number of that item and declaring the new value.

Let's look at the example below:

X = ["string1", "string2", "string3", "string4", "string5",
"string6"]
X [3] = "newstring"
print (X)

OUTPUT – ["string1", "string2", "string3", "newstring,"
"string5", "string6"]

You can also determine the **length** of a Python List using the
"len()" function, as shown in the example below:

X = ["string1", "string2", "string3", "string4", "string5",
"string6"]
print (len (X))

OUTPUT – 6

Python Lists can also be changed by **adding new items** to an
existing list using the built-in "append ()" method, as shown in
the example below:

X = ["string1", "string2", "string3", "string4"]
X.append ("newstring")
print (X)

OUTPUT – ["string1", "string2", "string3", "string4", "newstring"]

You can also, add a new item to an existing Python List at a specific position using the built-in "insert ()" method, as shown in the example below:

X = ["string1", "string2", "string3", "string4"]
X.insert (2, "newstring")
print (X)

OUTPUT – ["string1", "string2", "newstring", "string4"]

There might be instances when you need to **copy** an existing Python List. This can be accomplished by using the built-in "copy ( )" method or the "list ( )" method, as shown in the example below:

X = ["string1", "string2", "string3", "string4", "string5", "string6"]
Y = X.copy( )
print (Y)

OUTPUT – ["string1", "string2", "string3", "string4", "string5", "string6"]

X = ["string1", "string2", "string3", "string4", "string5", "string6"]

Y = list (X)

print (Y)

OUTPUT – ["string1", "string2", "string3", "string4", "string5", "string6"]

There are multiple built-in methods to **delete items** from a Python List.

- To selectively delete a specific item, the "remove ()" method can be used.

  X = ["string1", "string2", "string3", "string4"]

  X.remove ("string2")

  print (X)

  OUTPUT - ["string1", "string3", "string4"]

- To delete a specific item from the List, the "pop ()" method can be used with the position of the value. If no index has been indicated, the last item of the index will be removed.

  X = ["string1", "string2", "string3", "string4"]

  X.pop ( )

  print (X)

  OUTPUT - ["string1", "string2", "string3"]

- To delete a specific index from the List, the "del ()" method can be used, followed by the index within square brackets.

  X = ["string1", "string2", "string3", "string4"]

  del X [2]

print (X)

OUTPUT - ["string1", "string2", "string4"]

- To delete the entire List variable, the "del ()" method can be used, as shown below.

X = ["string1", "string2", "string3", "string4"]

del X

OUTPUT - .....

- To delete all the string values from the List without deleting the variable itself, the "clear ()" method can be used, as shown below.

X = ["string1", "string2", "string3", "string4"]

X.clear()

print (X)

OUTPUT – [ ]

Concatenation of Lists

You can join multiple lists with the use of the "+" logical operator or by adding all the items from one list to another using the "append ( )" method. The "extend ( )" method can be used to add a list at the end of another list. Let's look at the examples below to understand these commands.

```
X = ["string1", "string2", "string3", "string4"]
Y = [10, 20, 30, 40]

Z = X + Y
print (Z)
```

OUTPUT – ["string1", "string2", "string3", "string4", 10, 20, 30, 40]

```
X = ["string1", "string2", "string3", "string4"]
Y = [10, 20, 30, 40]

For x in Y:
        X.append (x)

print (X)
```

OUTPUT – ["string1", "string2", "string3", "string4", 10, 20, 30, 40]

```
X = ["string1", "string2", "string3"]
Y = [10, 20, 30]

X.extend (Y)
print (X)
```

OUTPUT – ["string1", "string2", "string3", 10, 20, 30]

EXERCISE – Create a list "A" with string data values as "red, green, blue, purple, yellow" and display the item at -2 position.
USE YOUR DISCRETION HERE AND WRITE YOUR CODE FIRST

Now, check your code against the correct code below:

A = ["red", "green", "blue", "purple", "yellow"]
print (A [-2])

OUTPUT – ["purple"]

EXERCISE – Create a list "A" with string data values as "red, green, blue, purple, yellow" and display the items ranging from the string on the second position to the end of the string.
USE YOUR DISCRETION HERE AND WRITE YOUR CODE FIRST

Now, check your code against the correct code below:

A = ["red", "green", "blue", "purple", "yellow"]
print (A [2 :])

OUTPUT – ["red", "teal", "blue", "purple", "yellow"]

EXERCISE – Create a list "A" with string data values as "red, green, blue, purple, yellow" and replace the string "green" to "teal."

USE YOUR DISCRETION HERE AND WRITE YOUR CODE FIRST

Now, check your code against the correct code below:

```
A = ["red", "green", "blue", "purple", "yellow"]
A [1] = ["teal"]

print (A)
```

OUTPUT – ["blue", "purple", "yellow"]

EXERCISE – Create a list "A" with string data values as "red, green, blue, purple, yellow" and copy the list "A" to create list "B."

USE YOUR DISCRETION HERE AND WRITE YOUR CODE FIRST

Now, check your code against the correct code below:

```
A = ["red", "green", "blue", "purple", "yellow"]
B = A.copy ( )
```

print (B)

OUTPUT – ["red", "green", "blue", "purple", "yellow"]

EXERCISE – Create a list "A" with string data values as "red, green, blue, purple, yellow" and delete the strings "red" and "purple."

USE YOUR DISCRETION HERE AND WRITE YOUR CODE FIRST

Now, check your code against the correct code below:

A = ["red", "green", "blue", "purple", "yellow"]
del.A [0, 2]
print (A)

OUTPUT – ["green", "blue", "yellow"]

Python Tuples

In Python, Tuples are collections of data types that cannot be changed but can be arranged in specific order. Tuples allow for duplicate items and are written within round brackets, as shown in the syntax below.

Tuple = ("string1", "string2", "string3")
print (Tuple)

Similar to the Python List, you can selectively display the desired string from a Tuple by referencing the position of that string inside square bracket in the print command as shown below.

Tuple = ("string1", "string2", "string3")
print (Tuple [1])

OUTPUT – ("string2")

The concept of **negative indexing** can also be applied to Python Tuple, as shown in the example below:
Tuple = ("string1", "string2", "string3", "string4", "string5")
print (Tuple [-2])

OUTPUT – ("string4")

You will also be able to specify a **range of indexes** by indicating the start and end of a range. The result in values of such command on a Python Tuple would be a new Tuple containing only the indicated items, as shown in the example below:

Tuple = ("string1", "string2", "string3", "string4", "string5",
"string6")
print (Tuple [1:5])
OUTPUT – *("string2", "string3", "string4", "string5")*
* Remember the first item is at position 0 and the final position
of the range, which is the fifth position in this example, is not
included.

You can also specify a **range of negative indexes** to Python
Tuples, as shown in the example below:

Tuple = ("string1", "string2", "string3", "string4", "string5",
"string6")
print (Tuple [-4: -2])

OUTPUT – *("string4", "string5")*

* Remember the last item is at position -1 and the final position
of this range, which is the negative fourth position in this
example is not included in the Output.

Unlike Python lists, you cannot directly **change the data
value of Python Tuples** after they have been created.
However, conversion of a Tuple into a List and then modifying
the data value of that List will allow you to subsequently create a
Tuple from that updated List. Let's look at the example below:

Tuple1 = ("string1", "string2", "string3", "string4", "string5",
"string6")
List1 = list (Tuple1)
List1 [2] = "update this list to create new tuple"
Tuple1 = tuple (List1)

print (Tuple1)

OUTPUT – ("string1", "string2", "update this list to create new
tuple", "string4", "string5", "string6")
You can also determine the **length** of a Python Tuple using the
"len()" function, as shown in the example below:

Tuple = ("string1", "string2", "string3", "string4", "string5",
"string6")
print (len (Tuple))

OUTPUT – 6

You cannot selectively delete items from a Tuple, but you can
use the "del" keyword to **delete the Tuple** in its entirety, as
shown in the example below:

Tuple = ("string1", "string2", "string3", "string4")
del Tuple

print (Tuple)

OUTPUT – name 'Tuple' is not defined

You can **join multiple Tuples** with the use of the "+" logical operator.

Tuple1 = ("string1", "string2", "string3", "string4")
Tuple2 = (100, 200, 300)

Tuple3 = Tuple1 + Tuple2
print (Tuple3)

OUTPUT – ("string1", "string2", "string3", "string4", 100, 200, 300)

You can also use the "tuple ( )" constructor to create a Tuple, as shown in the example below:

Tuple1 = tuple (("string1", "string2", "string3", "string4"))
print (Tuple1)

EXERCISE – Create a Tuple "X" with string data values as "peas, carrots, broccoli, onion, potato" and display the item at -3 position.

Now, check your code against the correct code below:

X = ("peas," "carrots," "broccoli," "onion," "potato")
print (X [-3])

OUTPUT – ("broccoli")

EXERCISE – Create a Tuple "X" with string data values as "peas, carrots, broccoli, onion, potato" and display items ranging from -2 to -4.

*** USE YOUR DISCRETION HERE AND WRITE YOUR CODE FIRST***

Now, check your code against the correct code below:

X = ("peas," "carrots," "broccoli," "onion," "potato")
print (X [-4 : -2])

OUTPUT – ("carrots," "broccoli")

EXERCISE – Create a Tuple "X" with string data values as "peas, carrots, broccoli, onion, potato" and change it's item from "potato" to "tomato" using List function.

USE YOUR DISCRETION HERE AND WRITE YOUR CODE FIRST*

Now, check your code against the correct code below:

X = ("peas", "carrots", "broccoli", "onion", "potato")
Y = list (X)
Y [4] = "tomato"
X = tuple (Y)

print (X)

OUTPUT – ("peas," "carrots," "broccoli," "onion," "tomato")

EXERCISE – Create a Tuple "X" with string data values as "peas, carrots, potato" and another Tuple "Y" with numeric data values as (2, 12, 22), then join them together.

USE YOUR DISCRETION HERE AND WRITE YOUR CODE FIRST*

Now, check your code against the correct code below:

X = *("peas," "carrots," "potato")*

Y = *(2, 12, 22)*

Z = *X* + *Y*

print (Z)

OUTPUT – ("peas," "carrots," "potato," 2, 12, 22)

Python Sets

In Python, Sets are collections of data types that cannot be organized and indexed. Sets do not allow for duplicate items and must be written within curly brackets, as shown in the syntax below.

set = *{"string1", "string2", "string3"}*

print (set)

Unlike the Python List and Tuple, you cannot selectively display desired items from a Set by referencing the position of that item because the Python Set are not arranged in any order. Therefore, items do not have any indexing. However, the "for" loop can be used on Sets (more on this topic later in this chapter).

Unlike Python Lists, you cannot directly **change the data values of Python Sets** after they have been created. However, you can use the "add ()" method to add a single item to Set and use the "update ( )" method to one or more items to an already existing Set. Let's look at the example below:

set = {"string1", "string2", "string3"}
set. add ("newstring")
print (set)
OUTPUT – {"string1", "string2", "string3", "newstring"}

set = {"string1", "string2", "string3"}
set. update (["newstring1", "newstring2", "newstring3",)
print (set)

OUTPUT – {"string1", "string2", "string3", "newstring1", "newstring2", "newstring3"}

You can also determine the **length** of a Python Set using the "len()" function, as shown in the example below:

set = {"string1", "string2", "string3", "string4", "string5", "string6", "string7"}
print (len(set))

OUTPUT – 7

To selectively **delete a specific item from a Set**, the "remove ()" method can be used as shown in the code below:

```
set = {"string1", "string2", "string3", "string4", "string5"}
set. remove ("string4")
print (set)
```

OUTPUT – {"string1", "string2", "string3", "string5"}
You can also use the "discard ( )" method to delete specific items
from a Set, as shown in the example below:

```
set = {"string1", "string2", "string3", "string4", "string5"}
set. discard ("string3")
print (set)
```

OUTPUT – {"string1", "string2", "string4", "string5"}
The "pop ( )" method can be used to selectively delete only the
last item of a Set. It must be noted here that since the Python
Sets are unordered, any item that the system deems as the last
item will be removed. As a result, the output of this method will
be the item that has been removed.

```
set = {"string1", "string2", "string3", "string4", "string5"}
A = set.pop ( )
print (A)
print (set)
```

OUTPUT –

String2

{"string1", "string3", "string4", "*string5*"}

To delete the entire Set, the "del" keyword can be used, as shown below.

set = {"string1", "string2", "string3", "string4", "string5"}
delete set
print (set)

OUTPUT – name 'set' is not defined

To delete all the items from the Set without deleting the variable itself, the "clear ()" method can be used, as shown below.

set = {"string1", "string2", "string3", "string4", "string5"}
set.clear ( )
print (set)

OUTPUT – set ( )

You can **join multiple Sets** with the use of the "union ( )" method. The output of this method will be a new set that contains all items from both the sets. You can also use the "update ( )" method to insert all the items from one set into another without creating a new Set.

Set1 = {"string1", "string2", "string3", "string4", "string5"}
Set2 = {15, 25, 35, 45, 55}
Set3 = Set1.union (Set2)
print (Set3)

OUTPUT – {"string1", 15, "string2", 25, "string3", 35, "string4", 45, "string5", 55}

Set1 = {"string1", "string2", "string3", "string4", "string5"}
Set2 = {15, 25, 35, 45, 55}
Set1.update (Set2)
print (Set1)

OUTPUT – {25, "string1", 15, "string4",55, "string2", 35, "string3", 45, "string5"}

You can also use the "set ( )" constructor to create a Set, as shown in the example below:

Set1 = set (("string1", "string2", "string3", "string4", "string5"))
print (Set1)

OUTPUT – {"string3", "string5", "string2", "string4", "string1"}

EXERCISE – Create a Set "Veg" with string data values as "peas, carrots, broccoli, onion, potato" and add new items "tomato," "celery" and "avocado" to this Set.

*****USE YOUR DISCRETION HERE AND WRITE YOUR CODE FIRST*****

Now, check your code against the correct code below:

Veg = {"peas," "carrots," "broccoli," "onion," "potato"}
Veg.update (["tomato," "celery," "avocado"])
print (Veg)

OUTPUT – {"peas," "celery," "onion," "carrots," "broccoli," "avocado," "potato," "tomato"}

EXERCISE – Create a Set "Veg" with string data values as "peas, carrots, broccoli, onion, potato," then delete the last item from this Set.

*****USE YOUR DISCRETION HERE AND WRITE YOUR CODE FIRST*****

Now, check your code against the correct code below:

Veg = {"peas", "carrots", "broccoli", "onion", "potato"}

```
X = Veg.pop ( )
print (X)
print (Veg)
```

OUTPUT –
broccoli
{"peas," "onion," "carrots," "potato"}

EXERCISE – Create a Set "Veg" with string data values as "peas, carrots, broccoli, onion, potato" and another Set "Veg2" with items as "tomato, eggplant, celery, avocado." Then combine both these Sets to create a third new Set.

USE YOUR DISCRETION HERE AND WRITE YOUR CODE FIRST

Now, check your code against the correct code below:

```
Veg = {"peas," "carrots," "broccoli," "onion," "potato"}
Veg2 = {"tomato", "eggplant", "celery", "avocado"}

AllVeg = Veg.union (Veg2)        #this Set name may vary as it
has not been defined in the exercise

print (AllVeg)
```

OUTPUT – {"peas", "celery", "onion", "carrots", "eggplant", "broccoli", "avocado", "potato", "tomato"}

Python Dictionary

In Python, Dictionaries are collections of data types that can be changed and indexed but are not arranged in any order. Each item in a Python Dictionary will comprise a key and its value. Dictionaries do not allow for duplicate items and must be written within curly brackets, as shown in the syntax below.

dict = {
"key1": "value1",
"key2": "value2",
"key3": "value3",
}
print (dict)

You can selectively display desired item value from a Dictionary by referencing its key inside square brackets in the print command as shown below.

dict = {
"key1": "value1",
"key2": "value2",

"key3": "value3",
}

X = dict ["key2"]
print (X)

OUTPUT – value2

You can also use the "get ( )" method to view the value of a key, as shown in the example below:

dict = {
"key1": "value1",
"key2": "value2",
"key3": "value3",
}

X = dict.get ("key1")
print (X)

OUTPUT – value1

There might be instances when you need to **change the value** of a key in a Python Dictionary. This can be accomplished by referring to the key of that item and declaring the new value. Let's look at the example below:

```
dict = {
"key1": "value1",
"key2": "value2",
"key3": "value3",
}
```

```
dict ["key3"] = "NEWvalue"
print (dict)
```

OUTPUT – {"key1": "value1", "key2": "value2", "key3": "NEWvalue"}

You can also determine the **length** of a Python Dictionary using the "len()" function, as shown in the example below:

```
dict = {
"key1": "value1",
"key2": "value2",
"key3": "value3",
"key4": "value4",
"key5": "value5"
}
```

```
print (len (dict))
```

OUTPUT – 5

Python Dictionary can also be changed by **adding** new index key and assigning a new value to that key, as shown in the example below:

dict = {
"key1": "value1",
"key2": "value2",
"key3": "value3",
}

dict ["NEWkey"] = "NEWvalue"
print (dict)

OUTPUT – {"key1": "value1", "key2": "value2", "key3": "value3", "NEWkey": "NEWvalue"}

There are multiple built-in methods to **delete items** from a Python Dictionary.

- To selectively delete a specific item value, the "pop ()" method can be used with the indicated key name.

  dict = {
  "key1": "value1",
  "key2": "value2",
  "key3": "value3",

```
}
dict.pop ("key1")
print (dict)
```

OUTPUT – { "key2": "value2", "key3": "value3"}

- To selectively delete the item value that was last inserted, the "popitem ()" method can be used with the indicated key name.

```
dict = {
"key1": "value1",
"key2": "value2",
"key3": "value3",
}
dict.popitem ( )
print (dict)
```

OUTPUT – { "key1": "value1", "key2": "value2"}

- To selectively delete a specific item value, the "del" keyword can also be used with the indicated key name.

```
dict = {
"key1": "value1",
"key2": "value2",
```

"key3": "value3",
}
del dict ("key3")
print (dict)

OUTPUT – { "key1": "value1", "key2": "value2"}

- To delete a Python Dictionary in its entirety, the "del" keyword can also be used as shown in the example below:

dict = {
"key1": "value1",
"key2": "value2",
"key3": "value3",
}
del dict
print (dict)

OUTPUT – name 'dict' is not defined

- To delete all the items from the Dictionary without deleting the Dictionary itself, the "clear ()" method can be used as shown below.

dict = {
"key1": "value1",
"key2": "value2",

"key3": "value3",

}

dict.clear ( )

print (dict)

OUTPUT – { }

There might be instances when you need to **copy** an existing Python Dictionary. This can be accomplished by using the built-in "copy ( )" method or the "dict ( )" method, as shown in the examples below:

dict = {
"key1": "value1",
"key2": "value2",
"key3": "value3",
}
newdict = dict.copy ( )
print (newdict)

OUTPUT – {"key1": "value1", "key2": "value2", "key3": "value3"}

Olddict = {
"key1": "value1",
"key2": "value2",
"key3": "value3",
}

newdict = dict (Olddict)

print (newdict)

OUTPUT – {"key1": "value1", "key2": "value2", "key3": "value3"}

There is a unique feature that supports multiple Python Dictionaries to be **nested** within another Python Dictionary. You can either create a Dictionary containing child Dictionaries, as shown in the example below:

```
McDonaldFamilyDict = {
        "burger1" : {
                "name" : "McPuff",
                "price" : 2.99
        },
        "burger2" : {
                "name" : "BigMac",
                "price" : 5
        },
        "burger3" : {
                "name" : "McDouble",
                "price" : 1.99

        }
}
print (McDonaldFamilyDict)
```

OUTPUT - {"burger1" : { "name" : "McPuff", "price" : 2.99}, "burger2" : {"name" : "BigMac", "price" : 5}, "burger3" : {"name" : "McDouble", "price" : 1.99}}

Or you can create a brand new Dictionary that contain other Dictionaries already existing on the system; your code will look like the one below:

```
burgerDict1 : {
        "name" : "McPuff,"
        "price" : 2.99
}

burgerDict2 : {
        "name" : "BigMac",
        "price" : 5
}

burgerDict3 : {
        "name" : "McDouble",
        "price" : 1.99
}

McDonaldFamilyDict = {
        "burgerDict1" : burgerDict1,
        "burgerDict2" : burgerDict2
```

```
        "burgerDict3" : burgerDict3
}
print (McDonaldFamilyDict)
```

OUTPUT - {"burger1" : { "name" : "McPuff", "price" : 2.99},
"burger2" : {"name" : "BigMac", "price" : 5}, "burger3" : {"name"
: "McDouble", "price" : 1.99}}

Lastly, you can use the "dict ( )" function to create a new Python
Dictionary. The key differences when you create items for the
Dictionary using this function are 1. Round brackets are used
instead of the curly brackets. 2. Equal to sign is used instead of
the semi-colon. Let's look at the example below:

*DictwithFunction = dict (key1 = "value1", key2 = "value2", key3
= "value3")*
print (DictwithFunction)

OUTPUT – {"key1": "value1", "key2": "value2", "key3": "value3"}

EXERCISE – Create a Dictionary "Starducks" with items
containing keys as "type," "size" and "price" with corresponding
values as "latte," "grande" and "4.99". Then add a new item with
key as "syrup" and value as "hazelnut."

USE YOUR DISCRETION HERE AND WRITE YOUR CODE FIRST

Now, check your code against the correct code below:

```
Starducks = {
"type" : "latte",
"size" : "grande",
"price" : 4.99
}
Starducks ["syrup"] = "hazelnut"
print (Starducks)
```

OUTPUT – {"type" : "latte", "size" : "grande", "price" : 4.99, "syrup" : "hazelnut"}

EXERCISE – Create a Dictionary "Starducks" with items containing keys as "type," "size," and "price" with corresponding values as "latte," "grande" and "4.99". Then use a function to remove the last added item.

USE YOUR DISCRETION HERE AND WRITE YOUR CODE FIRST

Now, check your code against the correct code below:

```
Starducks = {
"type" : "latte",
"size" : "grande",
"price" : 4.99
}
Starducks.popitem ( )
print (Starducks)
```

OUTPUT – {"type" : "latte", "size" : "grande"}

EXERCISE – Create a Dictionary "Starducks" with nested dictionary as listed below:

Dictionary Name	Key	Value
Coffee1	name	latte
	size	venti
Coffee2	name	espresso
	size	grande
Coffee3	name	mocha
	size	small

USE YOUR DISCRETION HERE AND WRITE YOUR CODE FIRST

Now, check your code against the correct code below:

```
Starducks = {
```

```
        "coffee1" : {
                "name" : "latte",
                "size" : "venti"
        },
        "coffee2" : {
                "name" : "espresso",
                "size" : "grande"
        },
        "coffee3" : {
                "name" : "mocha",
                "size" : "small"
        }
}
print (Starducks)
```

OUTPUT - {"coffee1" : { "name" : "latte", "size" : "venti"}, "coffee2" : {"name" : "espresso", "size" : "grande"}, "coffee3" : {"name" : "mocha", "size" : "small"}}

EXERCISE – Use the "dict ()" function to create a Dictionary "Starducks" with items containing keys as "type," "size" and "price" with corresponding values as "latte," "grande" and "4.99".

*****USE YOUR DISCRETION HERE AND WRITE YOUR CODE FIRST*****

Now, check your code against the correct code below:

Starducks = dict (type = "latte", size = "grande", price = 4.99}
print (Starducks)

OUTPUT – {"type" : "latte", "size" : "grande", "price" : 4.99,
"syrup" : "hazelnut"}

Python Conditions and If statement

Python allows the usage of multiple mathematical, logical
conditions as listed below:

- Equal to – "x == y"
- Not equal – "x !=y"
- Less than – "x < y"
- Less than, equal to – "x <= y"
- Greater than – "x > y"
- Greater than, equal to – "x >=y"

If Statement

All these conditions can be used within loops and **"if
statement"**. The "if" keyword must be used to write these
statements, as shown in the syntax below:

X = numeric1
Y = numeric2

```
if X > Y:
        print ("X is greater than Y")
```

The most important thing to remember here is that the indentation or the blank space at the beginning of a line in the code above is critical. Unlike other programming languages that use curly brackets, Python programming is driven by indentation in the process of defining the scope of the code. Therefore, writing the Python code below will result in an error.

```
X = numeric1
Y = numeric2
if X > Y:
print ("X is greater than Y")       #leads to an error
```

Else-if Statement

You can use the "elif" keyword to evaluate if the preceding condition is not true, then execute the subsequent condition. Here is the syntax followed by an example to help you understand this concept further:

```
X = numeric1
Y = numeric2
if X > Y:
        print ("X is greater than Y")
```

elif X == Y:

    print ("X and Y are equal")

Example:

X = 58

Y = 58

if X > Y:

    print ("X is greater than Y")

elif X == Y:

    print ("X and Y are equal")

OUTPUT - X and Y are equal

Else Statement

You can use the "else" keyword to execute any condition if the preceding conditions are not true.
Here is the syntax followed by an example to help you understand this concept further:

X = numeric1

Y = numeric2

if X > Y:

    print ("X is greater than Y")

elif X == Y:

```
        print ("X and Y are equal")
else:
        print ("Y is greater than X")
```

Example:

```
X = 58
Y = 59
if X > Y:
        print ("X is greater than Y")
elif X == Y:
        print ("X and Y are equal")
else:
        print ("Y is greater than X")
```

OUTPUT - Y is greater than X

Alternatively, you can use the "else" keyword without using the "elif" keyword, as shown in the example below:

```
X = 69
Y = 96
if X > Y:
        print ("X is greater than Y")
else:
        print ("X is not greater than Y")
```

OUTPUT - X is not greater than Y

Single Line If Statement

You could even execute single line statements with "If" clause, as shown in the syntax below:

If x > y: print ("y is greater than x")

Single Line If-Else Statement

You could even execute single line statements with "If - Else" clause, as shown in the syntax below:

x = 10
y = 15
print ("x") If x > y else print ("y")

Single Line If-Else Statement with multiple Else

You will also be able to execute single line statements with "If - Else" clause containing multiple "Else" statements in the same line, as shown in the syntax below:

x = 100
y = 100
print ("x") If x > y else print ("=") if a == b else print ("y")

"And" Keyword

If you are looking to combine multiple conditional statements, you can do so with the use of the "and" keyword, as shown in the example below:

$x = 20$

$y = 18$

$z = 35$

if $x > y$ and $z > x$:

      print ("All conditions are True")

"Or" Keyword

If you are looking to combine multiple conditional statements, the other way you can do so is with the use of the "or" keyword, as shown in the example below:

$x = 20$

$y = 18$

$z = 35$

if $x > y$ or $x > z$:

      print ("At least one of the conditions is True")

"Nested If" Statements

You can have multiple "if" statements within an "if" statement, as shown in the example below:

```
x = 110

if x > 50:
        print ("Greater than 50, ")
if x > 90:
        print ("and greater than 100")
else:
        print ("Not greater than 100")
```

"Pass" statements

In Python, if you ever need to execute "if" statements without any content, you must incorporate a "pass" statement to avoid triggering any error. Here is an example to further your understanding of this concept.

```
x = 20
y = 55
if y > x
    pass
```

EXERCISE – Write the code to check if X = 69 is greater than Y = 79, the output should read "X is greater than Y." If the first condition is not true, then check if X is equal to Y, the output should read "X and Y are equal" otherwise the output should read "Y is greater than X."

Now, check your code against the correct code below:

```
X = 69
Y = 79
if X > Y:
        print ("X is greater than Y")
elif X == Y:
        print ("X and Y are equal")
else:
        print ("Y is greater than X")
```

OUTPUT – "Y is greater than X"

EXERCISE – Write the code to check if x = 69 is greater '50', the output should read "Greater than 50". Then check if x is greater than '60', the output should read "And greater than 60", otherwise the output should read "Not greater than 60".

Now, check your code against the correct code below:

x = 69

```
if x > 50:
        print ("Greater than 50")
if x > 60:
        print ("And greater than 60")
else:
        print ("Not greater than 60")
```

OUTPUT –

"Greater than 50"

"And greater than 60"

EXERCISE – Write the code to check if x = 9 is greater than y = 19 as well as if z = 25 is greater than x. The output should read if one or both the conditions are true.

USE YOUR DISCRETION HERE AND WRITE YOUR CODE FIRST

Now, check your code against the correct code below:

```
x = 9
y = 19
z = 25
if x > y and z > x :
```

print ("Both the conditions are True")

OUTPUT – "Both the conditions are True"

EXERCISE – Write the code to check if x = 45 is less than y = 459 or z = 1459 is less than x. The output should read if one or both the conditions are true.

USE YOUR DISCRETION HERE AND WRITE YOUR CODE FIRST

Now, check your code against the correct code below:

x = 45
y = 459
z = 1459
if x < y and z < x :
        print ("At least one of the conditions is True")

OUTPUT – "At least one of the conditions is True"

Python "While" Loop

Python allows the usage of one of its standard loop commands i.e. "while" loop for execution of a block of statements, given that the initial condition holds true.

Here is the syntax for "while" loop statements:

p = num1

while p < num2:

    print (p)

    p += 1

In the syntax above, to prevent the loop from continuing with no end, the variable (p) was limited by setting to an increment. It is a pre-requisite for the "while" loop to index the variable in the statement.

"break" statements

These statements allow exiting from the "while" loop, even if the set condition holds true. In the example below, the variable will exit the loop when it reaches 4:

p = 2

while p < 7:

    print (p)

    if p == 4

      break

    p += 2

OUTPUT –

2

3

4

"continue" statements

These statements allow the system to stop the execution of the current condition and move to the next iteration of the loop. In the example below, system will continue the execution of the subsequent command if the variable equals 2:

```
p = 1
while p < 5:
        p += 1
        if p == 2:
            continue
        print (p)
```

OUTPUT –

1

3

4

5

(Note - The number 2 is missing from the result above)

"else" statement

The "else" statement allows you to execute a set of code after the "while" condition doesn't hold true any longer. The output in the example below will include a statement that the initial condition is no longer true:

```
p = 1
while p < 5:
```

print (p)

p += 1

else:

print ("p is no longer less than 5")

OUTPUT –

1

2

3

4

p is no longer less than 5

EXERCISE – Write the code to print a series of number if x = 1 is smaller than 7.

USE YOUR DISCRETION HERE AND WRITE YOUR CODE FIRST

Now, check your code against the correct code below:

x = 1

while x < 7:

print (x)

x += 1

OUTPUT –

1

2

3

4

5

6

EXERCISE – Write the code to print a series of number if x = 1 is smaller than 6 and exit the loop when x is 3.

USE YOUR DISCRETION HERE AND WRITE YOUR CODE FIRST

Now, check your code against the correct code below:

x = 1
while x < 6:
      print (x)
      if x == 3
        break
      x += 1

OUTPUT –

1

2

3

EXERCISE – Write the code to print a series of number if x = 1 is smaller than 6 and continue to execute the initial condition if x is 3 in a new iteration.

USE YOUR DISCRETION HERE AND WRITE YOUR CODE FIRST

Now, check your code against the correct code below:

```
x = 1
while x < 6:
        x += 1
        if x == 3:
        continue
        print (x)
```

OUTPUT –

1

2

4

5

6

(Note – The number 3 is missing, but the initial condition is executed in a new iteration.)

EXERCISE – Write the code to print a series of number if x = 1 is smaller than 4. Once this condition turns false, print "x is no longer less than 4".

USE YOUR DISCRETION HERE AND WRITE YOUR CODE FIRST

Now, check your code against the correct code below:

```
x = 1
while x < 4:
        print (x)
        x = 1
else:
        print ("x is no longer less than 4")
```

OUTPUT –

1

2

3

x is no longer less than 4

Python "For" Loop

Another one of the Python standard loops is "for" loop, which is used to execute iterations over a series such as string, tuple, set, dictionary, list. The "for" keyword in Python functions like an iterator found in object-oriented programming languages. It allows the execution of a block of statements once for every single item of tuple, set, list, and other series.

Let's look at the example below:

```
veg = ["tomato," "onion," "potato"]
for X in veg:
        print (X)
```

OUTPUT –
tomato
onion
potato

You will notice that in the code above that the variable was not defined. The "for" loop can be executed without setting an index for the variable in the code.

Loops for String

Python strings constitute a series of characters are iterative in nature. So if you wanted to loop through characters of a string, you could simply use the "for" loop as shown in the example below:

```
for X in "carrot":
        print (X)
```

OUTPUT –

c

a

r

r

o

t

"break" statements

If you want to exit the loop prior to its completion, you can use the "break" statements as shown in the example below:

```
veg = ["tomato," "onion," "potato," "peas," "carrot"]
for X in veg:
        print (X)
        if X == "peas":
        break
```

OUTPUT –

tomato

onion

potato

peas

In the example below, the print command was executed prior to the "break" statement and directly affected the output:

```
veg = ["tomato," "onion," "potato," "peas," "carrot"]
for X in veg:
        if X == "peas":
                break
        print (X)
```

OUTPUT –
tomato
onion
potato

"continue" statement

Similar to the "while" loop, the "continue" statements in the "for" loop is used to stop the execution of the current condition and move to the next iteration of the loop. Let's looks at the example below to further understand this concept:

```
veg = ["tomato," "onion," "potato," "peas," "carrot"]
for X in veg:
        if X == "potato":
                continue
        print (X)
```

OUTPUT –

tomato

onion

peas

carrot

"range" function

The "range ( )" function can be used to loop through a block of code for a specific number of times. This function will result in a series of number beginning with "0" by default, with regular increments of 1 and ending at a specific number.

Here is an example of this function:

for X in range (5):
        print (X)

OUTPUT –

0

1

2

3

4

Note – The "range ( )" function defaulted to 0 as the first output, and the final value of the range, 5, is excluded from the output.

Let's look at another example with a start and end value of the "range ( )" function:

for X in range (1, 5):
        print (X)

OUTPUT –

1

2

3

4

In the example below, we will specify the increment value, which is set to 1 by default:

for X in range (3, 20, 5):
        print (X)

OUTPUT –

3

8

13

18

"Else" in "For" Loop

You can use the "else" keyword to specify a set of code that need to be executed upon the completion of the loop, as shown in the example below:

for X in range (5):

   print (X)

else:

   print ("The loop was completed")

OUTPUT –

0

1

2

3

4

The loop was completed

"Nested" Loops

When loops are defined within a loop, execution of the inner loop will occur once for each iteration of the outer loop. Let's look at the example below, where we want every single adjective must be printed for each listed vegetable:

adjective = ["green," "leafy," "healthy"]

veg = ["spinach," "kale," "asparagus"]

```
for X in adjective:
    for Y in veg:
        print (X, Y)
```

OUTPUT –

green spinach

green kale

green asparagus

leafy spinach

leafy kale

leafy asparagus

healthy spinach

healthy kale

healthy asparagus

"pass" statements

In Python, if you ever need to execute "for" loops without any content, you must incorporate a "pass" statement to avoid triggering any error. Here is an example to further your understanding of this concept.

```
for X in [ 1, 2, 3]
    pass
```

OUTPUT - ......

The empty "for" loop code above would have resulted in an error without the "pass" statement.

EXERCISE – Write the code to loop through a list of colors ("blue," "purple," "red") without defining a variable. Then loop through the characters of the string "blue."

USE YOUR DISCRETION HERE AND WRITE YOUR CODE FIRST

Now, check your code against the correct code below:

colors = ["blue," "purple," "red"]
for A in colors:
        print (A)
for B in "blue":
        print (B)

OUTPUT –
blue
purple
red
b
l
u
e

EXERCISE – Write the code to loop through a list of colors ("blue," "purple," "red," "white") without defining a variable. Then break the loop at "red," without printing it in the result.

USE YOUR DISCRETION HERE AND WRITE YOUR CODE FIRST*

Now, check your code against the correct code below:

```
colors = ["blue", "purple", "red", "white"]
for A in colors:
        if A == "red":
            break
        print (A)
OUTPUT –
blue
purple
```

EXERCISE – Write the code to loop through a range of numbers starting with 5 and ending with 30. Make sure to define the increments at 6.

USE YOUR DISCRETION HERE AND WRITE YOUR CODE FIRST*

Now, check your code against the correct code below:

```
for X in range (5, 30, 6):
        print (X)
```

OUTPUT –

5

11

16

22

28

EXERCISE – Write the code to loop phones ("iPhone," "Samsung," "Google"), and loop that with colors ("black," "white," "gold") using nested loops.

USE YOUR DISCRETION HERE AND WRITE YOUR CODE FIRST

Now, check your code against the correct code below:

```
colors = ["black," "white," "gold"]
phones = ["iPhone," "Samsung," "Google"]

for X in colors:
        for Y in phones:
        print (X, Y)
```

OUTPUT –
black iPhone
black Samsung
black Google
white iPhone
white Samsung
white Google
gold iPhone
gold Samsung
gold Google

Chapter 3: Data Analysis and Machine Learning with Python

In 2001, Gartner defined Big data as "Data that contains greater variety arriving in increasing volumes and with ever-higher velocity." This led to the formulation of the "three V's." Big data refers to an avalanche of structured and unstructured data that is endlessly flooding and from a variety of endless data sources. These data sets are too large to be analyzed with traditional analytical tools and technologies but have a plethora of valuable insights hiding underneath.

The "Vs" of Big data

Volume – To be classified as big data, the volume of the given data set must be substantially larger than traditional data sets. These data sets are primarily composed of unstructured data with limited structured and semi structured data. The unstructured data or the data with unknown value can be collected from input sources such as web pages, search history, mobile applications, and social media platforms. The size and customer base of the company is usually proportional to the volume of the data acquired by the company.

Velocity – The speed at which data can be gathered and acted upon the first to the velocity of big data. Companies are increasingly using combination of on-premise and cloud-based servers to increase the speed of their data collection. The modern-day "Smart Products and Devices" require real-time access to consumer data, in order to be able to provide them a more engaging and enhanced user experience.

Variety – Traditionally a data set would contain majority of structured data with low volume of unstructured and semi-structured data, but the advent of big data has given rise to new unstructured data types such as video, text, audio that require sophisticated tools and technologies to clean and process these data types to extract meaningful insights from them.

Veracity – Another "V" that must be considered for big data analysis is veracity. This refers to the "trustworthiness or the quality" of the data. For example, social media platforms like Facebook and Twitter with blogs and posts containing hashtags, acronyms and all kinds of typing errors can significantly reduce the reliability and accuracy of the data sets.

Value – Data has evolved as a currency of its own with intrinsic value. Just like traditional monetary currencies, the ultimate value of the big data is directly proportional to the insight gathered from it.

History of Big Data

The origin of large volumes of data can be traced back to the 1960s and 1970s when the Third Industrial Revolution had just started to kick in, and the development of relational databases had begun along with construction of data centers. But the concept of big data has recently taken center stage primarily since the availability of free search engines like Google and Yahoo, free online entertainment services like YouTube and social media platforms like Facebook. In 2005, businesses started to recognize the incredible amount of user data being generated through these platforms and services, and in the same year and open-source framework called "Hadoop", was developed to gather and analyze these large data dumps available to the companies. During the same period non-relational or distributed database called "NoSQL", started to gain popularity due to its ability to store and extract unstructured data. "Hadoop" made it possible for the companies to work with big data with high ease and at a relatively low cost.

Today with the rise of cutting edge technology, not only humans but machines also generating data. The smart device technologies like "Internet of things" (IoT) and "Internet of systems" (IoS) have skyrocketed the volume of big data. Our everyday household objects and smart devices are connected to the Internet and able to track and record our usage patterns as well as our interactions with these products and feeds all this data directly into the big data. The advent of machine learning technology has further increased the volume of data generated on a daily basis. It is estimated that by 2020, "1.7 MB of data will be generated per second per person." As the big data will continue to grow, it usability still has many horizons to cross.

Importance of big data

To gain reliable and trustworthy information from a data set, it is very important to have a complete data set which has been made possible with the use of big data technology. The more data we have, the more information and details can be extracted out of it. To gain a 360 view of a problem and its underlying solutions, the future of big data is very promising. Here are some examples of the use of big data:

Product development – Large and small e-commerce businesses are increasingly relying upon big data to understand customer demands and expectations. Companies can develop predictive models to launch new products and services by using primary characteristics of their past and existing products and services and generating a model describing the relationship of those characteristics with commercial success of those products and services. For example, a leading fast manufacturing commercial goods company Procter & Gamble extensively uses big data gathered from the social media websites, test markets and focus groups in preparation for their new product launch.

Predictive maintenance – In order to besides leave project potential mechanical and equipment failures, a large volume of unstructured data such as error messages, log entries, and normal temperature of the machine must be analyzed along with available structured data such as make and model of the equipment and year of manufacturing. By analyzing this big data set using the required analytical tools, companies can extend the shelf life of their equipment by preparing for scheduled maintenance ahead of time and predicting future occurrences of potential mechanical failures.

Customer experience – The smart customer is aware of all of the technological advancements and is loyal only to the most engaging and enhanced user experience available. This has triggered a race among the companies to provide unique customer experiences analyzing the data gathered from customers' interactions with the company's products and services. Providing personalized recommendations and offers to reduce customer churn rate and effectively kind words prospective leads into paying customers.

Fraud and compliance – Big data helps in identifying the data patterns and assessing historical trends from previous fraudulent transactions to effectively detect and prevent potentially fraudulent transactions. Banks, financial institutions, and online payment services like PayPal are constantly monitoring and gathering customer transaction data in an effort to prevent fraud.

Operational efficiency – With the help of big data predictive analysis. companies can learn and anticipate future demand and product trends by analyzing production capacity, customer feedback, and data pertaining to top-selling items and product Will result in to improve decision-making and produce products that are in line with the current market trends.

Machine learning – For a machine to be able to learn and train on its own it requires humongous volume of data, i.e. big data. A solid training set containing structured, semi-structured and unstructured data will help the machine to develop a multidimensional view of the real world and the problem it is engineered to resolve. (Details on machine learning will be provided later in this book.)

Drive innovation – By studying and understanding the relationships between humans and their electronic devices as well as the manufacturers of these devices, companies can develop improved and innovative products by examining current product trends and meeting customer expectations.

"The importance of big data doesn't revolve around how much data you have, but what you do with it. You can take data from any source and analyze it to find answers that enable 1) cost reductions, 2) time reductions, 3) new product development and optimized offerings, and 4) smart decision making."
- SAS

The functioning of big data

There are three important actions required to gain insights from big data:

Integration – The traditional data integration methods such as ETL (Extract, Transform, Load) are incapable of collating data from a wide variety of unrelated sources and applications that are you at the heart of big data. Advanced tools and technologies are required to analyze big data sets that are exponentially larger than traditional data sets. By integrating big data from these disparate sources, companies are able to analyze and extract valuable insight to grow and maintain their businesses.

Management – Big data management can be defined as "the organization, administration, and governance of large volumes of both structured and unstructured data." Big data requires efficient and cheap storage, which can be accomplished using servers that are on-premise, cloud-based or a combination of both. Companies are able to seamlessly access required data from anywhere across the world and then processing this is data using required processing engines on as-needed basis. The goal is to make sure the quality of the data is high-level and can be accessed easily by required tools and applications. Big data gathered from all kinds of Dale sources including social media platforms, search engine history and call logs. The big data usually contains large sets of unstructured data and semi-structured data, which are stored in a variety of formats. To be able to process and store this complicated data, companies require more powerful and advanced data management software beyond the traditional relational databases and data warehouse platforms.

New platforms are available in the market that are capable of combining big data with the traditional data warehouse systems in a "logical data warehousing architecture." As part of this effort, companies are required to make decisions on what data must be secured for regulatory purposes and compliance, what data must be kept for future analytical purposes, and what data has no future use and can be disposed of. This process is called "data classification," which allows rapid and efficient analysis of subset of data to be included in immediate decision-making process of the company.

Analysis – Once the big data has been collected and is easily accessible, it can be analyzed using advanced analytical tools and technologies. This analysis will provide valuable insight and actionable information. Big data can be explored to make new discoveries and develop data models using artificial intelligence and machine learning algorithms.

Big Data Analytics – The terms of big data and big data analytics are often used interchangeably, going to the fact that the inherent purpose of big data is to be analyzed. "Big data analytics" can be defined as a set of qualitative and quantitative methods that can be employed to examine large amounts of unstructured, structured, and semi-structured data to discover data patterns and valuable hidden insights. Big data analytics is the science of analyzing big data to collect metrics, key performance indicators, and Data trends that can be easily lost in the flood of raw data, buy using machine learning algorithms and automated analytical techniques. The different steps involved in "big data analysis" are:

Gathering Data Requirements – It is important to understand what information or data needs to be gathered to meet the business objective and goals. Data organization is also very critical for efficient and accurate data analysis. Some of the categories in which the data can be organized are gender, age, demographics, location, ethnicity, and income. A decision must also be made on the required data types (qualitative and quantitative) and data values (can be numerical or alphanumerical) to be used for the analysis.

Gathering Data – Raw data can be collected from disparate sources such as social media platforms, computers, cameras, other software applications, company websites, and even third-party data providers. The big data analysis inherently requires large volumes of data, majority of which is unstructured with a limited amount of structured and semi structured data. Data organization and categorization – Depending on the company's infrastructure Data organization could be done on a simple Excel spreadsheet or using and man tools and applications that are capable of processing statistical data. Data must be organized and categorized based on data requirements collected in step one of the big data analysis process.

Cleaning the data – To perform the big data analysis sufficiently and rapidly it is very important to make sure the data set is void of any redundancy and errors. Only a complete data set fulfilling the Data requirements must be proceeded to the final analysis step. Preprocessing of data is required to make sure the only high-quality data is being analyzed, and company resources are being put to good use.

"Big data is high-volume, and high-velocity and/or high-variety information assets that demand cost-effective, innovative forms of information processing that enable enhanced insight, decision making, and process automation."
- Gartner

Analyzing the data – Depending on the insight that is expected to be achieved by the completion of the analysis, any of the following four different types of big data analytics approach can be adopted:

Predictive analysis – This type of analysis is done to generate forecasts and predictions for future plans of the company. By the completion of predictive analysis on the company's big data, the future state of the company can be more precisely predicted and derived from the current state of the company. The business executives are keenly interested in this analysis to make sure the company day-to-day operations are in line with the future vision of the company. For example, to deploy advanced analytical tools and applications in the sales division of a company, the first step is to analyze the leading source of data. Once believes source analysis has been completed, the type and number of communication channels for the sales team must be analyzed. This is followed by the use of machine learning algorithms on customer data to gain insight into how the existing customer base is interacting with company's products or services. This predictive analysis will conclude with deployment of artificial intelligence-based tools to skyrocket the company's sales.

Prescriptive analysis – Analysis that is carried out by primarily focusing on the business rules and recommendations to generate selective analytical path as prescribed by the industry standards to boost company performance. The goal of this analysis is to understand the intricacies of various departments of the organization and what measures should be taken by the company to be able to gain insights from its customer data by using prescribed analytical pathway. This allows the company to embrace domain specificity and conciseness by providing sharp focus on it's existing and future big data analytics process.

Descriptive analysis – All the incoming data received and stored by the company can be analyzed to produce insightful descriptions on the basis of the results obtained. The goal of this analysis is to identify data patterns and current market trends that can be adopted by the company to grow their business. For example, credit card companies often require risk assessment results on all prospective customers to be able to make predictions on the likelihood of the customer failing to make their credit payments and make a decision whether the customer should be approved for the credit or not. This risk assessment it's primarily based on the customer's credit history but also takes into account other influencing factors, including remarks from other financial institutions that the customer had approached for credit, customer income, and financial performance as well as their digital footprint and social media profile.

Diagnostic analysis – As the name suggests this type of analysis is done to diagnose or understand why a certain event unfolded and how that event can be prevented from occurring in future or replicated if needed. For example, web marketing strategies and campaigns often employ social media platforms to get publicity and increase their goodwill. Not all campaigns are as successful as expected; therefore, learning from failed campaigns is just as important, if not more. Companies can run diagnostic analysis on their campaign by collecting data pertaining to the mentions on the social media of the campaign, number of campaign page views, the average amount of time spent on the campaign page by an individual, number of social media fans and followers of the campaign, online reviews and other related metrics to understand why the campaign failed and how future campaigns can be made more effective.

The big data analysis can be conducted using one or more of the tools listed below:

- Hadoop – Open source data framework.

- Python – Programming language widely used for machine learning.
- SAS – Advanced analytical tool used primarily for big data analysis.
- Tableau – Artificial intelligence-based tool used primarily for data visualization.
- SQL – Programming language used to extract data from relational databases.
- Splunk – Analytical tool used to categorize machine-generated data
- R-programming – Programming language used primarily for statistical computing.

Machine Learning

Machine Learning can be defined as a subsidiary of Artificial Intelligence technology driven by the hypothesis that machines are capable of learning from data by identifying patterns and making decisions with little to no human assistance. The science of machine learning was birthed as a theory that computers have the potential to self learn specific tasks without needing to be programmed, using a pattern recognition technique. As the machines are exposed to new data the ability to adapt independently is the iterative aspect of machine learning. They can learn from and train themselves with prior computations to generate credible and reproducible decisions and results.

146

Machine learning algorithms have been in use for much longer than one would think, but their enhanced capability to analyze "big data" by automatically applying highly complex and sophisticated mathematical calculations rapidly and repeatedly, has been developed recently.

Now the topic of machine learning is so "hot" that the academia, business world, and the scientific community have their own take on its definition. Here are some of the widely accepted definitions from select highly reputed sources:

- *"Machine learning is the science of getting computers to act without being explicitly programmed."* – Stanford University
- *"The field of Machine Learning seeks to answer the question, how can we build computer systems that automatically improve with experience, and what are the fundamental laws that govern all learning processes?"* – Carnegie Mellon University
- *"Machine learning algorithms can figure out how to perform important tasks by generalizing from examples."* – University of Washington
- *"Machine Learning, at its most basic, is the practice of using algorithms to parse data, learn from it, and then make a determination or prediction about something in the world."* – Nvidia

- *"Machine learning is based on algorithms that can learn from data without relying on rules-based programming."* – McKinsey.

Machine learning allows an analysis of large volumes of data and delivers faster and more accurate results. With proper training, this technology can allow organizations to identify profitable opportunities and business risks. Machine learning, in combination with cognitive technologies and artificial intelligence, tends to be even more effective and accurate in processing massive quantities of data. The machine learning algorithms can be categorized into four:

Supervised machine learning algorithms – These algorithms are capable of applying the lessons from the previous runs to new data set using labeled examples to successfully make predictions for future events. For example, a machine can be programmed with data points labeled as "F" (failed) or "S" (success). The learning algorithm will receive inputs with corresponding correct outputs and run a comparison of its own actual output against the expected or correct, in an attempt to identify errors that can be fixed to make the model more efficient and accurate. With sufficient training the algorithms are capable of providing 'targets' for any new data input through methods like regression, classification, prediction, and ingredient boosting. The analysis starts from a known training data set, and the machine learning algorithm then produces an "inferred function" to make future predictions pertaining to the output values. For example, supervised learning algorithm based system is smart enough to anticipate and detect the likelihood of fraudulent credit card transactions being processed.

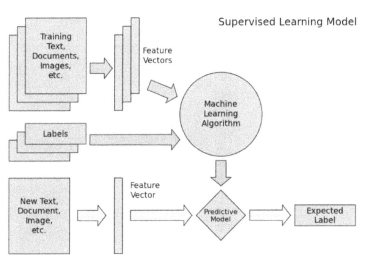

Unsupervised machine learning algorithms – These algorithms are used in the absence of classified and labeled training data sources. According to SAS, "Unsupervised Learning algorithms are used to study ways in which the system can infer a function to describe a hidden structure from unlabeled data, i.e. to explore the data and identify some structure within." Similar to the supervised learning algorithms, these algorithms are able to explore the data and draw inferences from data sets, but cannot figure out the right output.

For example, identification of individuals with similar shopping attributes, who can be segmented together and targeted with similar marketing campaigns. These algorithms are widely used to identify data outliers, provide product recommendations, and segment text topics using techniques like "singular value decomposition," "self-organizing maps," and "k-means clustering."

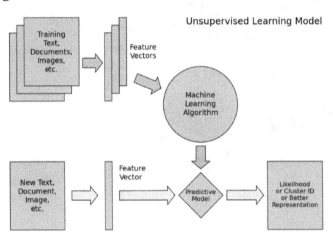

Semi-supervised machine learning algorithms – As the name indicates, these algorithms fall somewhere in between supervised and unsupervised learning and are capable of using labeled as well as unlabeled data as training sources. A typical training set would include a majority of the unlabeled data with a limited volume of the labeled data. The systems running on semi-supervised learning algorithms with methods such as prediction, regression, and classification are able to significantly improve their learning accuracy. In situations where the acquired labeled data requires relevant and skilled resources for the machine to be able to train or learn from it, the semi-supervised learning algorithms are best suited. For example, identification of individual faces on a web camera.

Reinforcement Machine learning algorithms – These algorithms are capable of interacting with their environment by producing actions and discovering errors or rewards. The primary characteristics of reinforcement learning are "trial and error research method and delayed reward." With the use of these algorithms machine can maximize its performance by automatically determining the ideal behavior within a specific context. The reinforcement signal is simply a reward feedback that is required by the machine or software agents to learn which actions yield fastest and accurate results. These algorithms are frequently used in robotics, gaming, and navigation.

Basic concepts of machine learning

The biggest draw of machine learning is the engineered capacity of the system to learn programs from the data automatically instead of manually constructing the program for the machine. Over the last decade the use of machine learning algorithms expanded from computer science to the industrial world. Machine learning algorithms are capable of generalizing tasks to execute them iteratively. The process of developing specific programs for specific tasks costs a lot of time and money, but occasionally it's just impossible to achieve. On the other hand, ML programming is often feasible and tends to be much more cost-effective. The use of machine learning in tackling ambitious issues of widespread importance, such as global warming and depleting underground water levels is promising with massive collection of relevant data.

"A breakthrough in machine learning would be worth ten Microsoft."
– Bill Gates

A number of types of machine learning exist today, but the concept of machine learning largely boils down to three components "representation," "evaluation" and "optimization." Here are some of the standard concepts that are applicable to all of them:

Representation

Machine learning models are incapable of directly hearing, seeing, or sensing input examples. Therefore, a data representation is required to supply the model with a useful vantage point into the key qualities of the data. To be able to successfully train a machine learning model selection of key features that best represent the data is very important. "Representation" simply refers to the act of "representing" data points to computer in a language that it understands using a set of classifiers. A classifier can be defined as "a system that inputs a vector of discrete and or continuous feature values and outputs a single discrete value called class." For a model to learn from the represented data the training data set or the "hypothesis space" must contain desired classifier that you want the models to be trained on. Any classifiers that are external to the hypothesis space cannot be learned by the model.

The data features used to represent the input are very critical to the machine learning process. The data features are so important to the development of desired machine learning model that it can easily be the difference between successful and failed machine learning projects. A training data set containing multiple independent features that are well correlated with the class can make the machine learning much smoother. On the other hand, class containing complex features may not be easy to learn from for the machine. This often requires the raw data to be processed so that desired features can be constructed from it, to be leveraged for the ML model. The process of deriving features from raw data tends to be the most time consuming and laborious part the ML project. It is also considered the most creative and interesting part of the project where intuition and trial and error play just as important role as the technical requirements.

The process of ML is not a one-shot process of developing a training data set and executing it instead it is an iterative process that requires analysis of the post-run output, followed by modification of the training data set and then repeating the whole process all over again. Another reason for the extensive time and effort required to engineer the training data set is domain specificity. Training data set for an e-commerce platform to generate predictions based on consumer behavior analysis will be very different from the training data set required to develop a self-driving car. However, the actual machine learning process remains largely the same across industrial domains. No wonder, a lot of research is being done to automate the feature engineering process.

Evaluation

Essentially the process of judging multiple hypotheses or models to choose one model over another is referred to as an evaluation. To be able to differentiate between useful classifiers from the vague ones an "evaluation function" is required. The evaluation function is also called as "objective," "utility" or "scoring" function. The machine-learning algorithm has its own internal evaluation function which tends to be different from the external evaluation function used by the researchers to optimize the classifier. Usually the evaluation function is defined prior to the selection of the data representation tool as the first step of the project. For example, the machine learning model for self-driving car has the feature for identification of pedestrians in its vicinity at near-zero false negatives and a low false-positive as an evaluation function and the pre-existing condition that needs to be "represented" using applicable data features.

Optimization

The process of searching the space of presented models to achieve better evaluations or highest-scoring classifier is called "optimization." For algorithms with more than one optimum classifier, the selection of optimization techniques is very critical in determination of the classifier produced and to achieve a more efficient learning model. A variety of off-the-shelf optimizers are available in the market to kick start new machine learning models before eventually replacing them with custom-designed optimizers.

Table 1. The three components of learning algorithms.

Representation	Evaluation	Optimization
Instances	Accuracy/Error rate	Combinatorial optimization
K-nearest neighbor	Precision and recall	Greedy search
Support vector machines	Squared error	Beam search
Hyperplanes	Likelihood	Branch-and-bound
Naive Bayes	Posterior probability	Continuous optimization
Logistic regression	Information gain	Unconstrained
Decision trees	K-L divergence	Gradient descent
Sets of rules	Cost/Utility	Conjugate gradient
Propositional rules	Margin	Quasi-Newton methods
Logic programs		Constrained
Neural networks		Linear programming
Graphical models		Quadratic programming
Bayesian networks		
Conditional random fields		

Machine Learning in Practice

The complete process of machine learning is much more extensive than just the development and application of machine learning algorithms and can be divided into steps below:

1. Define the goals of the project, taking into careful consideration all the prior knowledge and domain expertise available. Goals can easily become ambiguous since there are always additional things you want to achieve than practically possible to implement.

2. The data pre-processing and cleaning must result in a high-quality data set. This is the most critical and time-consuming step of the whole project. The larger the volume of data, the more noise it brings to the training

data set, which must be eradicated before feeding to the learner system.

3. Selection of appropriate learning model to meet the requirements of your project. This process tends to be rather simple, given the variety of types of data models available in the market.

4. Depending on the domain the machine learning model is applied to, the results may or may not require a clear understanding of the model by human experts as long as the model can successfully deliver desired results.

5. The final step is to consolidate and deploy the knowledge or information gathered from the model to be used on an industrial level.

6. The whole cycle from step 1 to 5 listed above is iteratively repeated until a result that can be used in practice is achieved.

Machine Learning Libraries

Machine learning libraries are sensitive routines and functions that are written in any given language. Software developers require a robust set of libraries to perform complex tasks without needing to rewrite multiple lines of code. Machine learning is largely based on mathematical optimization, probability, and statistics.

Python is the language of choice in the field of machine learning credited to consistent development time and flexibility. It is well suited to develop sophisticated models and production engines that can be directly plugged into production systems. One of its greatest assets being an extensive set of libraries that can help researchers who are less equipped with developer knowledge to easily execute machine learning.

"Scikit-Learn" has evolved as the gold standard for machine learning using Python, offering a wide variety of "supervised" and "unsupervised" ML algorithms. It is touted as one of the most user-friendly and cleanest machine learning libraries to date. For example, decision trees, clustering, linear and logistics regressions, and K-means. Scikit-learn uses couple of basic Python libraries: NumPy and SciPy and adds a set of algorithms for data mining tasks, including classification, regression, and clustering. It is also capable of implementing tasks like feature selection, transforming data and ensemble methods in only a few lines.

In 2007, David Cournapeau developed the foundational code of "Scikit-Learn" as part of a "Summer of code" project for "Google." Scikit-learn has become one of Python's most famous open-source machine learning libraries since its launch in 2007. But it wasn't until 2010 that Scikit-Learn was released for public use. Scikit-Learn is an open-sourced, and BSD licensed, data mining and data analysis tool used to develop supervise and unsupervised machine learning algorithms build on Python. Scikit-learn offers various ML algorithms such as "classification," "regression," "dimensionality reduction," and "clustering." It also offers modules for feature extraction, data processing, and model evaluation.

Designed as an extension to the "SciPy" library, Scikit-Learn is based on "NumPy" and "matplotlib," the most popular Python libraries. NumPy expands Python to support efficient operations on big arrays and multidimensional matrices. Matplotlib offers visualization tools and science computing modules are provided by SciPy. For scholarly studies, Scikit-Learn is popular because it has a well-documented, easy-to-use and flexible API. Developers are able to utilize Scikit-Learn for their experiments with various algorithms by only altering a few lines of the code. Scikit-Learn also provides a variety of training datasets, enabling developers to focus on algorithms instead of data collection and cleaning. Many of the algorithms of Scikit-Learn are quick and scalable to all but huge datasets. Scikit-learn is known for its reliability, and automated tests are available for much of the library. Scikit-learn is extremely popular with beginners in machine learning to start implementing simple algorithms.

Prerequisites for application of Scikit-Learn library

The Scikit-Learn library is based on the SciPy (Scientific Python), which needs to be installed before using SciKit-Learn. This stack involves the following:

NumPy (Base n-dimensional array package)

"NumPy" is the basic package with Python to perform scientific computations. It includes, among other things: "a powerful N-dimensional array object; sophisticated (broadcasting) functions; tools for integrating C/C++ and Fortran code; useful linear algebra, Fourier transform, and random number capabilities." NumPy is widely reckoned as effective multi-dimensional container of generic data in addition to its apparent scientific uses. It is possible to define arbitrary data types. This enables NumPy to integrate with a wide variety of databases seamlessly and quickly. The primary objective of NumPy is the homogeneity of multidimensional array. It consists of an element table (generally numbers), all of which are of the same sort and are indicated by tuples of non-negative integers. The dimensions of NumPy are called "axes" and array class is called "ndarray."

Matplotlib (Comprehensive 2D/3D plotting)

"Matplotlib" is a 2-dimensional graphic generation library from Python that produces high-quality numbers across a range of hardcopy formats and interactive environments. The "Python script," the "Python," "IPython shells," the "Jupyter notebook," the web app servers, and select user interface toolkits can be used with matplottib. Matplotlib attempts to further simplify easy tasks and make difficult tasks feasible. With only a few lines of code, you can produce tracks, histograms, scatter plots, bar graphs, error graphs, etc. □

A MATLAB-like interface is provided for easy plotting of the Pyplot Module, especially when coupled with IPython. As a power user, you can regulate the entire line styles, fonts properties, and axis properties through an object-oriented interface or through a collection of features similar to the one provided to MATLAB users.

SciPy (Fundamental library for scientific computing)
SciPy is a "collection of mathematical algorithms and convenience functions built on the NumPy extension of Python," capable of adding more impact to interactive Python sessions by offering high-level data manipulation and visualization commands and courses for the user. An interactive Python session with SciPy becomes an environment that rivals data processing and system prototyping technologies, including "MATLAB, IDL, Octave, R-Lab, and SciLab."

Another advantage of developing "SciPy" on Python, is the accessibility of a strong programming language in the development of advanced programs and specific apps. Scientific apps using SciPy benefit from developers around the globe, developing extra modules in countless software landscape niches. Everything produced has been made accessible to the Python programmer, from database subroutines and classes as well as "parallel programming to web." These powerful tools are provided along with the "SciPy" mathematical libraries.

IPython (Enhanced interactive console)

"IPython (Interactive Python)" is an interface or command shell for interactive computing using a variety of programming languages. "IPython" was initially created exclusively for Python, which supports introspection, rich media, shell syntax, tab completion, and history. Some of the functionalities provided by IPython include: "interactive shells (terminal and Qt-based); browser-based notebook interface with code, text, math, inline plots and other media support; support for interactive data visualization and use of GUI tool kits; flexible interpreters that can be embedded to load into your own projects; tools for parallel computing".

SymPy (Symbolic mathematics)

Developed by Ondřej Čertík and Aaron Meurer, SymPy is "an open-source Python library for symbolic computation." It offers algebra computing abilities to other apps, as a stand-alone app and/or as a library as well as live on the internet applications with "SymPy Live" or "SymPy Gamma." "SymPy" is easy to install and test, owing to the fact that it is completely developed in Python boasting limited dependencies. SymPy involves characteristics ranging from calculus, algebra, discrete mathematics, and quantum physics to fundamental symbolic arithmetic. The outcome of the computations can be formatted as "LaTeX" code. In combination with a straightforward, expandable codebase in a widespread programming language, the ease of access provided by SymPy makes it a computer algebra system with comparatively low entry barrier.

Pandas (Data structures and analysis)

Pandas provide highly intuitive and user-friendly high-level data structures. Pandas has achieved popularity in the machine learning algorithm developer community, with built-in techniques for data aggregation, grouping, and filtering as well as results of time series analysis. The Pandas library has two primary structures: one-dimensional "Series" and two-dimensional "Data Frames."

Seaborn (data visualization)

Seaborn is derived from the Matplotlib Library and an extremely popular visualization library. It is a high-level library that can generate specific kinds of graph including heat maps, time series, and violin plots.

Installing Scikit-Learn

The latest version of Scikit-Learn can be found on "Scikit-Learn.org" and requires "Python (version >= 3.5); NumPy (version >= 1.11.0); SciPy (version >= 0.17.0); joblib (version >= 0.11)". The plotting capabilities or functions of Scikit-learn start with "plot_" and require "Matplotlib (version >= 1.5.1)". Certain Scikit-Learn examples may need additional applications: "Scikit-Image (version >= 0.12.3), Pandas (version >= 0.18.0)".

With the prior installation of "NumPy" and "SciPy," the best method of installing Scikit-Learn is using "pip: pip install -U scikit-learn" or "conda: conda install scikit-learn."

One must make sure that "binary wheels" are utilized when using pip and that "NumPy" and "SciPy" have not been recompiled from source, which may occur with the use of specific OS and hardware settings (for example, "Linux on a Raspberry Pi"). Developing "NumPy" and "SciPy" from source tends to be complicated (particularly on Windows). Therefore, they need to be set up carefully, making sure optimized execution of linear algebra routines is achievable.

Application of machine learning using Scikit-Learn library

To understand how Scikit-Learn library is used in the development of machine learning algorithm, let us use the "Sales_Win_Loss data set from IBM's Watson repository" containing data obtained from sales campaign of a wholesale supplier of automotive parts. We will build a machine learning model to predict which sales campaign will be a winner and which will incur loss.

The data set can be imported using Pandas and explored using Pandas techniques such as "head(), tail(), and dtypes()." The plotting techniques from "Seaborn" will be used to visualize the data. To process the data Scikit-Learn's "preprocessing.LabelEncoder()" will be used and "train_test_split()" to divide the data set into training subset and testing subset.

To generate predictions from our data set, three different algorithms will be used, namely, "Linear Support Vector Classification and K-nearest neighbors classifier." To compare the performances of these algorithms Scikit-Learn library technique "accuracy_score" will be used. The performance score of the models can be visualized using Scikit-Learn and "Yellowbrick" visualization.

Importing the data set
To import the "Sales_Win_Loss data set from IBM's Watson repository," first step is importing the "Pandas" module using *"import pandas as pd."*

Then we leverage a variable url as *"https://community.watsonanalytics.com/wp content/uploads/2015/04/WA_Fn-UseC_-Sales-Win-Loss.csv"* to store the URL from which the data set will be downloaded.

Now, *"read_csv() as sales_data = pd.read_csv(url)"* technique will be used to read the above "csv or comma-separated values" file, which is supplied by the Pandas module. The csv file will then be converted into a Pandas data framework, with the result in variable as *"sales_data,"* where the framework will be stored.

For new 'Pandas' users, the *"pd.read csv()"* technique in the code mentioned above will generate a tabular data structure called "data framework", where an index for each row is contained in the first column, and the label / name for each column in the first row are the initial column names acquired from the data set. In the above code snippet, the *"sales data"* variable results in a table depicted in the picture below.

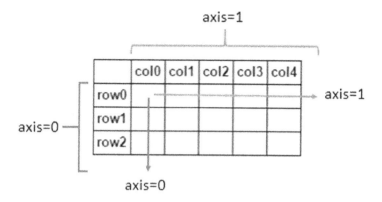

In the diagram above, the "row0, row1, row2" represents individual record index, and the "col0, col1, col2" represent the names for individual columns or features of the data set.

With this step, you have successfully stored a copy of the data set and transformed it into a "Pandas" framework!

Now, using the *"head() as Sales_data.head()"* technique, the records from the data framework can be displayed as shown below to get a "feel" of the information contained in the data set.

	opportunity number	supplies subgroup	supplies group	region	route to market	elapsed days in sales stage	opportunity result
0	1641984	Exterior Accessories	Car Accessories	Northwest	Fields Sales	76	Won
1	1658010	Exterior Accessories	Car Accessories	Pacific	Reseller	63	Loss
2	1674737	Motorcycle Parts	Performance & Non-auto	Pacific	Reseller	24	Won
3	1675224	Shelters & RV	Performance & Non-auto	Midwest	Reseller	16	Loss

Data Exploration

Now that we have our own copy of the data set, which has been transformed into a "Pandas" data frame, we can quickly explore the data to understand what information can tell can be gathered from it and accordingly to plan a course of action.

In any ML project, data exploration tends to be a very critical phase. Even a fast data set exploration can offer us significant information that could be easily missed otherwise, and this information can propose significant questions that we can then attempt to answer using our project.

Some third-party Python libraries will be used here to assist us with the processing of the data so that we can efficiently use this data with the powerful algorithms of Scikit-Learn. The same *"head()"* technique that we used to see some initial records of the imported data set in the earlier section can be used here. As a matter of fact, *"(head)"* is effectively capable of doing much more than displaying data records and customize the "head()" technique to display only a selected records with commands like *"sales_data.head(n=2)"*. This command will selectively display the first 2 records of the data set. At a quick glance it's obvious that columns such as "Supplies Group" and "Region" contain string data, while columns such as "Opportunity Result," "Opportunity Number" etc. are comprised of integer values. It can also be seen that there are unique identifiers for each record in the' Opportunity Number' column.

Similarly, to display select records from the bottom of the table, the *"tail() as sales_data.tail()"* can be used.

To view the different data types available in the data set, the Pandas technique *"dtypes() as sales_data.dtypes"* can be used. With this information, the data columns available in the data framework can be listed with their respective data types. We can figure out, for example, that the column "Supplies Subgroup" is an "object" data type and that the column "Client Size By Revenue" is an "integer data type." So, we have an understanding of columns that either contain integer values or string data.

Data Visualization

At this point, we are through with basic data exploration steps, so we will not attempt to build some appealing plots to portray the information visually and discover other concealed narratives from our data set.

Of all the available Python libraries providing data visualization features, "Seaborn" is one of the best available options, so we will be using the same. Make sure that python plots module provided by "Seaborn" has been installed on your system and ready to be used. Now follow the steps below generate desired plot for the data set:

Step 1 - Import the "Seaborn" module with command *"import seaborn as sns"*.

Step 2 - Import the "Matplotlib" module with command *"import matplotlib.pyplot as plt"*.

Step 3 - To set the "background colour" of the plot as white, use command *"sns.set(style="whitegrid", color_codes=True)"*.

Step 4 - To set the "plot size" for all plots, use command *"sns.set(rc={'figure.figsize':(11.7,8.27)})"*.

Step 5 – To generate a "countplot", use command *"sns.countplot('Route To Market',data=sales_data,hue = 'Opportunity Result')"*.

Step 6 – To remove the top and bottom margins, use command *"sns.despine(offset=10, trim=True)"*.

Step 7 – To display the plot, , use command *"plotplt.show()"*.

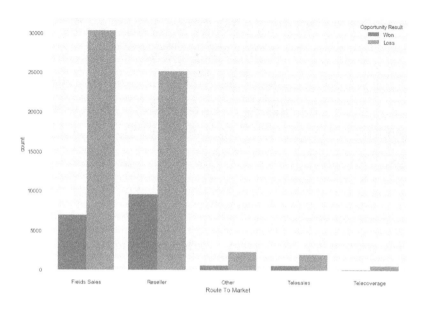

Quick recap - The "Seaborn" and "Matplotlib" modules were imported first. Then the *"set()"* technique was used to define the distinct characteristics for our plot, such as plot style and color. The background of the plot was defined to be white using the code snippet *"sns.set(style= "whitegrid," color codes= True)."* Then the plot size was define using command *"sns.set(rc={'figure.figsize':(11.7,8.27)})"* that define the size of the plot as "11.7px and 8.27px".

Next the command *"sns.countplot('Route To Market',data= sales data, hue='Opportunity Result')"* was used to generate the plot. The "countplot()" technique enables creation of a count plot, which can expose multiple arguments to customize the count plot according to our requirements. As part of the first

171

"*countplot()*" argument, the X-axis was defined as the column "Route To Market" from the data set. The next argument concerns the source of the data set, which would be "sales_data" data framework we imported earlier. The third argument is the color of the bar graphs that was defined as "blue" for the column labeled "won" and "green" for the column labeled "loss."

Data Pre-processing

By now you should have a clear understanding of what information is available in the data set. From the data exploration step, we established that majority of the columns in our data set are "string data," but "Scikit-Learn" can only process numerical data. Fortunately, the Scikit-Learn library offers us many ways to convert string data into numerical data, for example, "*LabelEncoder()*" technique. To transform categorical labels from the data set such as "won" and "loss" into numerical values, we will use the "*LabelEncoder()*" technique.

Let's look at the pictures below to see what we are attempting to accomplish with the "*LabelEncoder()*" technique. The first image contains one column labeled "color" with three records namely, "Red," "Green" and "Blue." Using the "*LabelEncoder()*" technique, the record in the same "color" column can be converted to numerical values, as shown in the second image.

	Color
0	Red
1	Green
2	Blue

	Color
0	1
1	2
2	3

Let's begin the real process of conversion now. Using the *"fit transform()"* technique given by *"LabelEncoder(),"* the labels in the categorical column like "Route To Market" can be encoded and converted to numerical labels comparable to those shown in the diagrams above. The function *"fit transform()"* requires input labels identified by the user and consequently Will result in encoded labels.

To know how the encoding is accomplished, let's go through an example quickly. The code instance below constitutes string data in the form of a list of cities such as ["paris," "paris," "tokyo," "amsterdam"] that will be encoded into something comparable to "[2, 2, 1,3]".

Step 1 - To import the required module, use command *"from sklearn import preprocessing."*
Step 2 – To create the Label encoder object, use command *"le = preprocessing.LabelEncoder()"*.
Step 3 – To convert the categorical columns into numerical values, use command:
"encoded_value = le.fit_transform(["paris", "paris", "tokyo", "amsterdam"])"

"print(encoded_value) [1 1 2 0]"

And there you have it! We just converted our string data labels into numerical values. The first step was importing the preprocessing module that offers the *"LabelEncoder()"* technique. Followed by development of an object representing the *"LabelEncoder()"* type. Then the *"fit_transform()"* function of the object was used to distinguish between distinct classes of the list ["paris," "paris," "tokyo," "amsterdam"] and output the encoded values of "[1 1 20]".

Did you observe that the *"LabelEncoder()"* technique assigned the numerical values to the classes in alphabetical order according to the initial letter of the classes, for example "(a)msterdam" was assigned code "0", "(p)aris" was assigned code "1" and "(t)okyo" was assigned code "2".

Creating Training and Test subsets

To know the interactions between distinct characteristics and how these characteristics influence the target variable, a ML algorithm must be trained on a collection of information. We need to split the complete data set into two subsets to accomplish this. One subset will serve as the training data set, which will be used to train our algorithm to construct machine learning models. The other subset will serve as the test data set, which will be used to test the accuracy of the predictions generate by the machine learning model.

The first phase in this stage is the separation of feature and target variables using the steps below:

Step 1 – To select data excluding select columns, use command *"select columns other than 'Opportunity Number', 'Opportunity Result'cols = [col for col in sales_data.columns if col not in ['Opportunity Number','Opportunity Result']]"*.
Step 2 – To drop these select columns, use command *"dropping the 'Opportunity Number'and 'Opportunity Result' columns*
data = sales_data[cols]".
Step 3 – To assign the Opportunity Result column as "target", use command *"target = sales_data['Opportunity Result'] data.head(n=2)"*.

The "Opportunity Number" column was removed since it just acts as a unique identifier for each record. The "Opportunity Result" contains the predictions we want to generate, so it becomes our "target" variable and can be removed from the data set for this phase. The first line of the above code will select all the columns except "Opportunity Number" and "Opportunity Result" in and assign these columns to a variable "cols." Then using the columns in the "cols" variable a new data framework was developed. This is going to be the "feature set." Next, the column "Opportunity Result" from the *"sales_data"* data frame was used to develop a new data framework called "target."

The second phase in this stage is to separate the date frameworks into training and testing subsets using the steps below. Depending on the data set and desired predictions, it needs to be split into training and testing subset accordingly. For this exercise, we will use 75% of the data as training subset, and rest 25% will be used for the testing subset. We will leverage the *"train_test_split()"* technique in "Scikit-Learn" to separate the data using steps and code as below:

Step 1 – To import required module, use command *"from sklearn.model_selection import train_test_split"*.
Step 2 – To separate the data set, use command *"split data set into train and test setsdata_train, data_test, target_train, target_test = train_test_split (data,target, test_size = 0.30, random_state = 10)"*.

With the code above, the *"train_test_split"* module was first imported, followed by the use of *"train_test_split()"* technique to generate "training subset *(data_train, target_train)"* and "testing subset *(data_test, data_train)."* The *"train_test_split()"* technique's first argument pertains to the features that were divided in the preceding stage; the next argument relates to the target ("Opportunity Result"). The third "test size" argument is the proportion of the data we wish to divide and use as testing subset. We are using 30% for this example, although it can be any amount. The fourth 'random state' argument is used to make sure that the results can be reproduced every time.

Building the Machine Learning Model

The "machine_learning_map" provided by Scikit-Learn is widely used to choose the most appropriate ML algorithm for the data set. For this exercise, we will be using "K-nearest neighbors classifier" algorithms.

K-nearest Neighbors Classifier

The "k-nearest neighbors(k-NN)" algorithm is referred to as "a non-parametric method used for classification and regression in pattern recognition." In cases of classification and regression, "the input consists of the nearest k closest training examples in the feature space." K-NN is form of "instance-based learning" or "lazy learning," in which the function is only locally estimated, and all calculations are delayed until classification. The output is driven by the fact, whether the classification or regression method is used for k-NN:

- "k-nearest neighbors classification" - The "output" is a member of the class. An "object" is classified by its neighbors' plurality vote, assigning the object to the most prevalent class among its nearest "k-neighbors," where "k" denotes a small positive integer. If k= 1, the "object" is simply allocated to the closest neighbor's class.

- "k-nearest neighbors regression" - The output is the object's property value, which is computed as an average of the k-nearest neighbor's values.

A helpful method for both classification and regression can be assigning weights to the neighbors' contributions, to allow closer neighbors to make more contributions in the average, compared to the neighbors located far apart. For instance, a known "weighting scheme" is to assign each neighbor a weight of "$1/d$", where "d" denotes the distance from the neighbor. The neighbors are selected from a set of objects for which the "class" (for "k-NN classification") or the feature value of the "object" (for "k-NN regression") is known.

Here are the steps and code for this algorithm to build our next ML model:

Step 1 – To import required modules, use command *"from sklearn.neighbors import KNeighborsClassifier"* and *"from sklearn.metrics import accuracy_score"*.

Step 2 – To create object of the classifier, use command *"neigh = KNeighborsClassifier(n_neighbors=3)"*.

Step 3 – To train the algorithm, use command *"neigh.fit(data_train, target_train)."*

Step 4 – To generate predictions, use command *"pred = neigh.predict(data_test)".*

Step 5 – To evaluate accuracy, use command *"print ('KNeighbors accuracy score:,' accuracy_score(target_test, pred))."*

With the code above, the required modules were imported in the first step. We then developed the object *"neigh"* of type "KNeighborsClassifier" with the volume of neighbors as *"n_neighbors=3"*. In the next step, the *"fit()"* technique was used to train the algorithm on the training data set. Next, the model was tested on the testing data set using *"predict()"* technique. Finally, the accuracy score was obtained, which could be *"KNeighbors accuracy score : 0.814550580998"*, for instance.

Now that our preferred algorithms have been introduced, the model with the highest accuracy score can be easily selected. But wouldn't it be great if we had a way to compare the distinct models' efficiency visually? In Scikit-Learn, we can use the "Yellowbrick library," which offers techniques for depicting various scoring techniques visually.

Python Tips and Tricks for Developers

Python was first implemented in 1989 and is regarded as highly user-friendly and simple to learn programming language for entry-level coders and amateurs. It is regarded ideal for individuals newly interested in programming or coding and need to comprehend programming fundamentals. This stems from the fact that Python reads almost the same as English language. Therefore, it requires less time to understand how the language works and focus can be directed in learning the basics of programming.

Python is an interpreted language that supports automatic memory management and object-oriented programming. This extremely intuitive and flexible programming language can be used for coding projects such as machine learning algorithms, web applications, data mining and visualization, game development.

Some of the tips and tricks you can leverage to sharpen up your Python programming skill set are:

In-place swapping of two numbers:

```
a, b = 101, 201
print (a, b)
a, b = b, a
print (a, b)"
```

180

Resulting Output =

101 201

201 101

Reversing a string:

a ="computer"

print ("Reverse is", a [::-1])

Resulting Output =

Reverse is retupmoc.

Creating a single string from multiple list elements:

a = ["this", "is", "learning","with", "passion"]

print (" ".join (a))

Resulting Output =

this is learning with passion

Stacking of comparison operators:

n = 101

result = 1 < n < 201

print (result)

result = 1 > n <= 91

print (result)

Resulting Output =
True
False

Print the file path of the imported modules:

import os;
import socket;

print(os)
print (socket

Resulting Output =
"<module 'os' from '/usr/lib/python3.5/os.py'>
<module 'socket' from '/usr/lib/python3.5/socket.py'>"

Use of enums in Python:

class MyName:
   Chic, For, Chic = range (3)
print (MyName.Chic)
print (MyName.For)
print (MyName.Chic)

Resulting Output =
2
1
2

Result in multiple values from functions:

def x ():

   result in 11, 21, 31, 41

a, b, c, d = x ()

print (a, b, c, d)

Resulting Output =

11 21 31 41

Identify the value with highest frequency:

test = [11, 21, 31, 41, 21, 21, 31, 11, 41, 41, 41]

print (max(set(test), key = test.count))

Resulting Output =

41

Check the memory usage of an object:

import sys

x = 1

print (sys.getsizeof (x))

Resulting Output =

28

Printing a string N times:

```
n = 2;
a ="ArtificialIntelligence";
print (a * n);
```

Resulting Output =
ArtificialIntelligenceArtificialIntelligenceArtificialIntelligence

Identify anagrams:

```
from collections import Counter
def is_anagram (str1, str2):
    result in Counter(str1) == Counter(str2)
print (is_anagram ('geek', 'eegk'))

print (is_anagram ('geek', 'reek'))
```

Resulting Output =
True
False

Transposing a matrix:

```
mat = [[11, 21, 31], [41, 51, 61]]
zip (*mat)
```

Resulting Output =
[(11, 41), (21, 51), (31, 61)]

Print a repeated string without using loops:

print "machine"*3+' '+"learning"*4

Resulting Output =

Machinemachinemachine learninglearninglearninglearning

Measure the code execution time:

import time

startTime = time.time()

"write your code or functions calls"

"write your code or functions calls"

endTime = time.time ()

totalTime = endTime – startTime

print ('Total time required to execute code is=' , totalTime)

Resulting Output =

Total time

Obtain the difference between two lists:

list1 = ['Brian', 'Pepper', 'Kyle', 'Leo', 'Sam']

list2 = ['Sam', 'Leo', 'Kyle']

set1 = set(list1)

set2 = set(list2)

list3 = list(set1.symmetric_difference(set2))

```
print(list3)
```

Resulting Output =
list3 = ['Brian', 'Pepper']

Calculate the memory being used by an object in Python:

```
import sys
list1 = ['Brian', 'Pepper', 'Kyle', 'Leo', 'Sam']
print ("size of list = ", sys.getsizeof(list1))
name = 'pynative.com'
print ('size of name =', sys.getsizeof(name))
```

Resulting Output =
('size of list = ', 112)
('size of name = ', 49)

Removing duplicate items from the list:

```
listNumbers = [20, 22, 24, 26, 28, 28, 20, 30, 24]
print ('Original=' , listNumbers)
listNumbers = list(set(listNumbers))
print ('After removing duplicate= ', listNumbers)
```

Resulting Output =
'Original= ', [20, 22, 24, 26, 28, 28, 20, 30, 24]
'After removing duplicate= ', [20, 22, 24, 26, 28, 30]

Find if a list contains identical elements:

listOne = [20, 20, 20, 20]

print ('All elements are duplicate in listOne',

listOne.count(listOne[0]) == len(listOne))

listTwo = [20, 20, 20, 50]

print ('All elements are duplicate in listTwo',

listTwo.count(listTwo[0]) == len(listTwo))

Resulting Output =

"'All elements are duplicate in listOne', True"

"'All elements are duplicate in listTwo', False"

Efficiently compare two unordered lists:

from collections import Counter

one = [33, 22, 11, 44, 55]

two = [22, 11, 44, 55, 33]

print ('is two list are b equal', Counter(one) == Counter(two))

Resulting Output =

"'is two list are b equal', True"

Check if list contains all unique elements:

def isUnique(item):

tempSet = set ()

result in not any (i in tempSet or tempSet.add(i) for i in item)

```
listOne = [123, 345, 456, 23, 567]
print ('All List elements are Unique', isUnique(listOne))
listTwo = [123, 345, 567, 23, 567]
print ('All List elements are Unique', isUnique(listTwo))
```

Resulting Output =
"All List elements are Unique True"
"All List elements are Unique False"

Convert Byte into String:

```
byteVar = b"pynative"
str = str (byteVar.decode ('utf-8'))
print ('Byte to string is', str )
```

Resulting Output =
"Byte to string is pynative"

Merge two dictionaries into a single expression:

```
currentEmployee = {1: 'Scott', 2: 'Eric', 3:'Kelly'}
formerEmployee = {2: 'Eric', 4: 'Emma'}
def merge_dicts(dictOne, dictTwo):
dictThree = dictOne.copy()
dictThree.update(dictTwo)
result in dictThree
print (merge_dicts (currentEmployee, formerEmployee))
```

Conclusion

Thank you for making it through to the end of *Learn Python: A Crash Course On Python Programming And How To Start Coding With It. Learn The Basics Of Machine Learning And Data Analysis*, let's hope it was informative and able to provide you with all of the tools you need to achieve your goals whatever they may be.

The next step is to make the best use of your new-found wisdom of Python programming, data analysis, and machine learning that have resulted in the birth of the powerhouse, which is the "Silicon Valley." Companies across the industrial spectrum with an eye on the future are gradually turning into Technology companies under the façade of their intended business model. This book is filled with real-life examples to help you understand the nitty-gritty of the concepts and names and descriptions of multiple tools that you can further explore and selectively implement to make sound choices for development of a desired machine learning model. Now that you have finished reading this book and mastered the use of Scikit-Learn you are all set to start developing your own Python machine learning model using all the open sources readily available and explicitly mentioned in this book for that purpose. You can position yourself to use your deep knowledge and understanding of machine learning technologies obtained from this book to contribute to the growth of any company and land yourself a new high paying and rewarding job!

Finally, if you found this book useful in any way, a review on Amazon is always appreciated!

www.ingramcontent.com/pod-product-compliance
Lightning Source LLC
Chambersburg PA
CBHW071123050326
40690CB00008B/1323